EMOTIONS AND FIELDWORK

SHERRYL KLEINMAN
MARTHA A. COPP
University of North Carolina

Qualitative Research Methods
Volume 28

SAGE PUBLICATIONS
International Educational and Professional Publisher
Newbury Park   London   New Delhi

For information address:

SAGE Publications, Inc.
2455 Teller Road
Newbury Park, California 91320
E-mail: order@sagepub.com

SAGE Publications Ltd.
6 Bonhill Street
London EC2A 4PU
United Kingdom

SAGE Publications India Pvt. Ltd.
M-32 Market
Greater Kailash I
New Delhi 110 048 India

Printed in the United States of America

Library of Congress Cataloging-in-Publication Data

Kleinman, Sherryl.
  Emotions and fieldwork / Sherryl Kleinman, Martha A. Copp.
      p.   cm. — (Qualitative research methods ; v. 28)
  Includes bibliographical references.
  ISBN 0-8039-4721-6. — ISBN 0-8039-4722-4 (pbk.)
    1. Social sciences—Fieldwork. 2. Sociology—Fieldwork.
  3. Social sciences—Fieldwork—Psychological aspects.
  4. Sociology—Fieldwork—Psychological aspects. 5. Emotions
  I. Copp, Martha A. II. Title. III. Series.
  H62.K585   1993
  300'.723—dc20   93-21683

              01 02 03 9 8 7 6 5 4

Sage Production Editor: Judith L. Hunter

CONTENTS

ACKNOWLEDGMENTS

Martha thanks Sherryl for making collaboration a joy from their first freewritings to the final editing. She appreciates the cooperative, inductive approach that Sherryl shared with her as mentor and then as colleague. Rekha Mirchandani, Kristin Park, and Audrey Vanden Heuvel supported Martha's grumbling and rejoicing over writing. She thanks Jeff Supplee for the same and also for his enthusiasm and emotional understanding. She received a summer graduate research stipend from the Institute for Research in Social Science at the University of North Carolina to work on the book.

Sherryl thanks Martha for her insights, conscientiousness, and good spirits. Most of all she appreciates Martha's willingness to move beyond the student role. Sherryl also thanks the members of her writing group— Jane Brown, Marcy Lansman, Erica Rothman, Len Stanley, and Fabienne Worth—for listening with care to her readings from the manuscript. Sociologizing across the miles with Martha McMahon and Barbara Rauschenbach helped her through snags. She is grateful to Michael Schwalbe for sharing his fieldwork stories, pointing out the "clunks" in her writing, and keeping her emotional life interesting.

We thank Broad St. Coffee Roasters in Carrboro and Foster's Market in Durham for making us feel at home during multiple-hour work-and-talk sessions. We thank Della Pollock, Dwight Rogers, Barbara Smalley, and Barbara Stenross for their thorough readings of the manuscript. Shea Farrell helped with the word processing. John Van Maanen supported us throughout the project. His incisive, witty commentary improved the process and the product.

EDITORS' INTRODUCTION

Fieldwork may be the most homespun of methods in the social sciences. It represents something of a scholarly Outward Bound Program and those who sign up sometimes take what seems to be an almost unnatural pride in its folksy, emergent, adventurous, and native-friendly image. Fieldwork is supposed to be fun. To the uninitiated, it may even appear as a wonderful rationale for having a good time under the cover of doing serious intellectual work. At times, enjoyment itself becomes a measure for success in the field. If one is keeping good company, learning good stuff, and having a good day, the work must be going well. Anger, boredom, confusion, disgust, self-doubt, depression, lust, despair, frustration, and embarrassment are perhaps more than occasionally associated with fieldwork, but they are not often discussed—at least not in print—because such sentiments violate the pleasure principle so often associated with model practice. To wit, fieldworkers who report liking or admiration for those they study will rarely be accused of bringing the wrong standards to bear on such judgments. But those who find fault with those they studied or admit to having had less than a splendid time in the field risk charges of having failed to properly grasp the native's point of view or, worse, will stand accused of rampant ethnocentrism. This curious policing of socially correct feeling within the fieldwork community can lead to a rather bizarre slanting of research reports wherein the fieldworker is represented as wallowing in an almost unmitigated delight while engaged in the research process. This is quite possibly one reason the actual experience of fieldwork can come as such a shock to the neophyte.

Such a shock might very well be reduced if we were to have at hand more forthcoming discussions of the broad range of emotions at play in fieldwork. This is the task taken up by Sherryl Kleinman and Martha A. Copp in Volume 28 of the Sage Qualitative Research Methods Series. *Emotions and Fieldwork* begins by taking the "unmitigated delight" version of fieldwork to task and ends by showing how qualitative studies might be improved by treating the feelings associated with fieldwork as worthy of more than a passing glance. And there is much to consider, for fieldwork, like any occupational endeavor, raises serious and certainly heartfelt questions about one's competence and self-identity, the worth of one's work, the moral responsibilities associated with the short- and long-term relations one develops with others in the field, the possible consequences—or lack thereof—of one's work, and so on (and on). Sorting out these forever shifting and puzzling emotions and coming to understand them in a way that adds depth, power, and character to the analysis of a fieldwork project is very much the achieved aim of this monograph.

In the final analysis, fieldwork is yet another addition to our repertoire of ways to make ourselves uncomfortable. It is perhaps a spectacular addition, too, because the fieldworker seeks to obtain something of a glacial clarity about an alien way of life by immersing him- or herself in the warm immediacies of that life. Emotional labor is thus central to the trade. But we might be made somewhat more comfortable if less of our efforts were devoted to the avoidance, denial, and control of emotions and if more of our efforts were directed to the understanding, expression, and reporting of them. More to the point of this monograph, however, is the plain fact that we can learn a good deal more from the field by treating our feelings as aids to analysis rather than hindrances.

—John Van Maanen
Peter K. Manning
Marc L. Miller

EMOTIONS AND FIELDWORK

SHERRYL KLEINMAN
MARTHA A. COPP
University of North Carolina

1. INTRODUCTION

Lacking awareness of [our] own emotional responses frequently re-
sults in [our] being more influenced by emotion rather than less.

Alison Jaggar
(1989, p. 158, emphasis added)

In this book we take a sociological look at fieldworkers' feelings and how
they relate to the research process. We use the symbolic interactionist
perspective (Blumer, 1969; Mead, 1934), especially where it informs the
growing subfield of the sociology of emotions. As symbolic inter-
actionists, we assume that emotions are social and cultural products but
that individuals have some control over them. As Arlie Hochschild (1983)
said, "Social factors enter not simply before and after but interactively
during the experience of emotion" (p. 211).

Our culture dictates feeling rules (Hochschild, 1983)—how we are supposed to feel in different situations—depending on our roles. For example,
we expect physicians to feel compassion, even sadness, for their dying
patients, but not to become depressed about them. In addition, we share
display rules—how we are supposed to express our feelings. We want

1

physicians to demonstrate concern for their patients through a caring glance or gesture, not through uncontrollable sobs.

Field researchers learn—through their teachers, texts, and colleagues—how to feel, think, and act. As members of the larger discipline, fieldworkers share a culture dominated by the ideology of professionalism or, more specifically, the ideology of science. According to that ideology, emotions are suspect. They contaminate research by impeding objectivity, hence they should be removed.

Field researchers also know that their feelings somehow affect their research. But do fieldworkers admit that they have feelings? Do they learn to take their feelings into account as they analyze their data? We suspect most would answer, "Not often." We doubt that others encourage fieldworkers to systematically reflect on their feelings throughout the research process. In addition, fieldworkers infer the value of emotions in their discipline by reading what their teachers consider important qualitative work. Classic ethnographies either omit researchers' emotions or relegate them to a preface or an appendix.

Qualitative researchers hear mixed messages. On one hand, they are told that their emotions can hinder good research. On the other, they are told that they will not understand participants unless they form attachments to them. Consequently, most of us act like quasi-positivists: We allow ourselves to have *particular* feelings, such as closeness with participants, and try to deny or get rid of emotions we deem inappropriate. Fieldworkers, then, do emotion work (Hochschild, 1983), molding their feelings to meet others' expectations.

In 1990, I (Sherryl) was asked to write an account of my experiences studying an alternative health organization (Kleinman, 1991). I found myself writing about the feelings I tried to ignore during the research and how they were now helping me analyze the data. At times I felt paralyzed by this study, even though I successfully completed other projects (e.g., Kleinman, 1984). This was my first experience of "analysis block." Several sociologists wrote to me after the chapter was published, thanked me for my honesty, and told me that my account had been therapeutic for them. Martha and I talked about why my story made such an impact. What stands in the way of our facing up to, or discussing with others, the feelings we experience in the field or at our desks? And what are the costs?

We will examine fieldworkers' feelings about their professional identity (chap. 2), their work (chap. 3), and the people they study (chap. 4). In the conclusion, we use an extended example from one of our field studies to highlight the points we raise in earlier chapters. The appendix demonstrates how to include feelings in fieldnotes. Throughout this volume, we discuss how the ideology of science shapes our research practices. By working in a profession infused with scientistic notions, field researchers inevitably lose—we compromise our studies and experience feelings of incompetence.

As fieldworkers, the practice of writing about field researchers without observing or interviewing them makes us uncomfortable. What are our data? In addition to our own experiences, we rely on published confessionals, some studies of anthropologists (Jackson, 1990a, 1990b), graduate students' accounts of their fieldwork experiences, and feedback from our colleagues.

We begin, then, by calling for a field study of fieldworkers, especially in sociology. Perhaps this kind of study is rare because we do not want to put our colleagues' (and our own) secrets into print (but see Platt, 1976). Perhaps we also fear that quantitative sociologists will find out the truth— that our work is as subjective as they suspected.

With our caveats in order, we now turn to our ruminations on emotions and fieldwork.

2. FIELDWORKERS AS PROFESSIONALS

Fieldworkers share some practices that are at odds with scientific canons. They mark us as different, even illegitimate, within the mainstream community. Despite these practices, positivistic assumptions inform many fieldworkers' beliefs and habits. In the first part of this chapter, we discuss the emotional costs of doing research in a context where the ideology of science predominates. In the second part of the chapter, we discuss the costs of conforming to science.

A Position of Vulnerability

Scientists are supposed to be experts: They control the research process. But qualitative researchers know that the success of our work depends on participants. As we phrased it in another manuscript, "Qualitative researchers only gain control of their projects by first allowing themselves to lose it" (Kleinman, Copp, & Henderson, 1992, p. 9). But how do we *feel* about losing control? A graduate student commented on an early set of her fieldnotes:

> What am I looking for? Sometimes I get a nervous pang in my stomach when I think to myself that this is so undirected, especially since I want to make a thesis out of it. . . . I must admit that I would feel better about it if I knew where I was going with it. . . . [I]t is always comforting to feel like you have some grounding. I feel like I'm floating now.

Experienced qualitative researchers, if writing honestly, would probably say something similar.

In this already vulnerable state, we may receive outright attacks about our practices, especially from those in other disciplines where qualitative research lacks acceptance. Within sociology, we often receive indirect challenges. Field researchers who work inductively dread their colleagues' innocuous query: "What is your research question?" If we interpret this as "What are you studying and why?" then we know we cannot give a satisfactory answer: "I am looking at the effect of X on Y."

We can reply that inductive researchers begin a project by assuming they know little (or have misinformation) about the setting and those in it. We can say that we have many questions and that these will change over time. We can say that an initial research question might prove useless on the first day in the field and better questions will emerge after we know more. But rather than dismiss this query, we feel uncomfortable and foolish. Hearing it confirms our fear that we do not know what we are doing and answering it makes us look incompetent to our colleagues. Because the "research question" changes even as we write the manuscript, our feelings of insecurity will continue for a long time.

Moreover, it may be just as difficult to explain why we chose a particular field site. Many field researchers cannot provide what is expected, that is, good theoretical reasons for observing people in this setting rather than in another, or interviewing people in this role rather than in another. Some of us have heard our mentors say, "It's not what you study but how you study it that matters." Yet we still worry about our motivation. Do we want to study this group because it might satisfy our voyeuristic desires? Or did we choose a familiar setting because we were afraid to approach a group that is different or threatening? Is there some other equally embarrassing reason? We (Kleinman et al., 1992) wrote elsewhere that "the best ideas for a particular project may begin in someone's offhand remark at the supermarket rather than in a sociological tome" (p. 7). But we feel better about ourselves when we know it came from a tome rather than the supermarket.

Like members of other minority groups, fieldworkers may appear defensive to those in the dominant group (or their aspirants). This has happened to us from time to time in our graduate seminars in fieldwork. For example, in the spring semester of 1992, after reading Herbert Blumer's (1969) spirited critique of much of quantitative sociology, a student in our class asked disdainfully why quantitative methodologists do not openly criticize qualitative methods. He scoffed, "They don't even mention it. But in courses in qualitative methods, quantitative methods *always* come up."

This student implied two things. First, he insinuated that qualitative sociologists are undermining themselves by taking quantitative methods into account (even if only to attack them). Second, quantitative sociologists, unlike qualitative sociologists, are civil human beings who do not say bad things about other kinds of work.

I (Sherryl) reacted to this upsetting comment by immediately offering a sociological explanation for the student's observation. I pointed out that the lack of critical remarks and the absence of any mention of qualitative research in "methods" courses indicate the hegemony of the quantitative approach. Were not his statistics professors making a strong statement about the place of qualitative methods by omitting them entirely? Qualitative researchers, then, have to legitimate their perspective to students in order to break the methodological silence coming from the other side.

Field researchers, unlike mainstream sociologists, are often substantively homeless. Most quantitative sociologists define themselves by particular substantive areas, such as medical sociology, criminology, or ethnic relations. They call their methods hats, which they put on or take off, depending on the particular research occasion. They may admit that they have some favorite hats, but still they assume that the research question determines the method. Fieldworkers, however, usually identify with their method because they see it as a perspective rather than a hat. We apply a set of orienting questions instead of a specific research question to different settings and substantive areas. We ask, for example, How do people shape, create and resist meanings? How does joint action emerge or dissipate or produce conflict? With a bag of general questions, we move across a wide variety of substantive areas.

But, in an era of specialization, others scorn our behavior and see us as dilettantes who flit from one area to the next. They may ask, Can you know enough about so many substantive areas to produce good work? Even if we argue that our focus is analytic rather than substantive—for example, that we are interested in professional socialization rather than in medical students or seminarians—we are less committed to the territories they hold dear. We charge onto their turf, change things around, and then leave without becoming part of their community. Others might not think of us as deserving the honorific title of the professional sociologist (Becker, 1970b).

Professional Expectations as a Liability

Our concerns for professional and emotional security influence our choices of what group or topic to study, where to study it, how long to study it, and how to tell others about it. Most of the time, we are unaware of these choices because we do not want to believe that we would succumb to professional pressures. Yet these unconscious concessions penalize our work.

YOU ARE WHAT YOU STUDY

Mainstream sociologists rank their topics (and units of analysis). Because researchers become identified with their areas of research, they think about which topics they want to be associated with. Like all professionals, sociologists learn which topics, populations, and areas are tainted (and thus should be avoided) and which are valued (and thus should be pursued) (Abbott, 1981).

Fieldworkers are supposed to be democratic about topics. They presumably share the belief that every setting yields a good story; we just need to be smart enough to make sense of it. Ideally, then, we esteem every well-done field study, regardless of topic. But fieldworkers, like other sociologists, make judgments about what deserves study and shift their assessments over time. We are especially sensitive to our colleagues' reactions at the start of a project. We want our topic to pique their curiosity.

To gain acceptance, fieldworkers may avoid areas that others consider unworthy or impure. We may find ourselves comparing our topic to those that meet current standards. Sometimes we are unaware that our setting has a stigma in the professional community until our colleagues and friends react to it. While studying violent criminals, Lonnie Athens (1989) found that the stigma of those he studied extended to himself, a researcher who could "establish rapport with such persons" (p. 20).

The value others place on our project affects how we feel about it and ourselves as fieldworkers. Although we are unlikely to attribute our feelings of boredom or anger at participants to our colleagues, their negative reactions may lead us to resent those we study. For example, during the late 1960s, many field researchers studied deviant groups. By the more conservative 1980s, fewer did. When I (Sherryl) studied an alternative health center in the early 1980s, I found myself feeling ambivalent about the study.

Initially, I was disappointed that the center was not as radical as I had expected. But the organization disappointed me in another way that speaks to the high value we currently place on conventional topics and settings. I felt cheated that the Wholeness Center was not a conventional establishment. Several quirky features of the organization made me feel uneasy: the small size of the organization (six practitioners working part-time), the type of building it was in (an old house), its financial instability, and the small number of clients. Was it a legitimate setting? Was it a real organization? These worries indicated that I accepted (albeit with some ambivalence) the conventional notions of organization shared by sociologists and lay people. As Mark Granovetter (1984) argued, most sociologists equate "organization" with formal, complex organizations. Even "complex" implies that a smaller organization is simple and therefore sociologically insignificant.

This bias against studying small, unconventional organizations extends beyond those who study formal organizations. One (usually openminded) sociologist said he thought it was time to study "normal organizations." Several sociologists told me they expected this type of organization to be flaky or fly-by-night. I was turned down for a small grant at my university because of such perceptions, which in turn made doing my work more difficult. These social scientists echoed my own concerns about the organization and my own doubts about whether I should study such a place.

I was doing what the other sociologists were doing: judging the sociological value of a study by the societal value of an organization or its value to sociologists at a given time. What I came to realize much later was that these critiques of the setting (and study) were also *data*. Our negative reactions reflected the society in which the Center was located and with which it had to struggle, a society where assumptions about legitimacy run deep. Significantly, I discovered that Wholeness Center members, too, had internalized some of these views. If I had left others' reactions at the level of criticisms rather than data, I would not have had the insights that later enriched my analysis.

Fieldworkers may feel ambivalent, as I did, about a group or setting that is not easily classified as deviant or mainstream. Some of our classic studies focused on unconventional groups: William Foote Whyte's (1955) gang, Howard Becker's (1963) marijuana smokers, Ned Polsky's (1967) hustlers. The sociology of deviance is less popular today, but studying deviant groups still fits our notion that fieldwork is an exciting adventure (see chap. 3) that takes us into hidden pockets of society.

Fieldworkers also get points for studying conventional organizations, as Rosabeth Kanter (1977) did for her study of a corporation. The in-between organizations, such as the Wholeness Center, lose on both counts: They lack the allure of deviant groups and the representativeness of main-stream organizations. Yet, in every study, we must figure out what the setting or group represents. Even studies of deviant behavior often suggest that participants are just like everyone else, hence their actions represent social behavior in general rather than deviant behavior alone. (The topics themselves, however, retain some glamour.) Because we do not know what sociological story the project will yield until later, we make life unnecessarily hard for ourselves and others when we judge the merits of a study by its topic.

FEELING PRESSED FOR TIME

Most field researchers agree that fieldwork, when done right, takes time. While others are doing secondary analysis on a large data set already accessible by computer, we are just beginning to collect data. Qualitative research is more difficult to compartmentalize than quantitative work and may take longer to write and publish. The emotional involvement of field-work usually spills over into the rest of our lives. Even when we do intermittent fieldwork, we often find ourselves thinking about the project at odd hours or culling data from newspapers and magazines. We may not live with those we study, but sometimes it feels as if they are living inside our heads.

Fieldwork *should* take time. How else can we produce well-written analyses that reflect the complexity of social life? But professional life in academia is rarely organized to help us get our work done, and so we become anxious about how we spend our time. Faculty members often tell graduate students to move quickly through the program. Most faculty refrain from saying "Don't collect your own data," but students get the message. Similarly, we have met faculty members in tenure track positions who tell us that they would like to do qualitative work, but they wonder whether others would take that work seriously, "and anyway, it takes too long." Others tell us they want to get themselves "settled" before they undertake qualitative research; they (correctly) perceive the risks.

Yet fieldworkers, like other professionals, expect their work performances to improve with each project and to become easier and faster over time. This probably happens as we grow comfortable with previously uncomfortable aspects of the role. Perhaps we adjust to the uncertainty and ambiguity inherent in the work. But, in our experience, the better we get at field research, the more difficult it becomes. For example, if we have successfully analyzed participants' talk in one project, we will develop some confidence. But a new setting may prompt us to analyze rituals and silences rather than words. This new learning slows us down. Similarly, as we get better at understanding how strands of meaning become themes in our data, more of them seem to appear. Our standards change, and we want the current analysis to reflect the kinds of complexities we feel we lacked in earlier projects. Yet the demands on our time have increased and we are supposed to know, as good professionals do, how to be efficient. What do we do?

We may decide to study a group familiar to us, perhaps one in which we already participate. We hope that familiarity will save us time and prevent the anxiety of entering a strange environment. This contradicts some fieldworkers' belief that it is best to study a less familiar group because we are likely to take the familiar for granted (but see Lofland & Lofland, 1984).

Or perhaps we choose an easily accessible group. We pick a site that fits our institutional schedule rather than our fieldworker curiosity. Some field researchers believe they lack the energy and time it takes to negotiate with human subjects committees or to complete a lengthy fieldwork project. For example, Diana Scully (1990) spent a year trying to accommodate the demands of three separate administrative bodies, each concerned with protecting the rights of the incarcerated rapists she had proposed to study. Consequently, some field researchers turn to intensive interviewing instead of participant observation. But, in doing so, the researcher may feel like less of a fieldworker. As we will explore in the next chapter, the fieldworker identity is grounded in immersion—getting lost in the data and collecting a massive data set. When we lack an experience of immersion, we may feel inauthentic.

MORE THAN JUST A RESEARCHER

The conventional image of a researcher is someone who neutralizes his or her "irrelevant" identities and viewpoints while conducting research. For example, Jean Jackson (1986) and Mary Ellen Conaway (1986) used to believe that anthropologists could transcend gender: "Both women and men studied for and practiced fieldwork, and these exercises seemed to carry them outside the common categories of gender- and sex-defined behavior" (Conaway, 1986, p. 52). But having a professional identity allows us to ignore that we enact a variety of social identities in the field. As Alan Peshkin (1988) discovered in his study of a fundamentalist Christian school, he could not be "the non-Christian scholar" (p. 275). He found that "being Jewish . . . became the unavoidably salient aspect of [his] subjectivity" (pp. 275-276).

Fieldworkers enter the field as more than researchers. Our identities and life experiences shape the political and ideological stances we take in our research. As Elizabeth Fee (1988) put it, "The idea of a pure knowing mind outside history is simply an epistemological conceit" (p. 53). Ignoring the interplay of person and research ultimately has analytic costs.

For example, when I (Sherryl) studied a seminary (Kleinman, 1984), I was conscious of the danger of ignoring the social identities and beliefs that I held. I worried about being an agnostic Jew studying devout Chrisians. Instead, being a nonreligious Jew added to the appeal I held for the ministry students. Additionally, I was conscious of my gender. I was surprised at the high proportion of female students (about 30%) and examined how these women prepared to join a male-dominated profession.

But I was not conscious of my race as an important identity. Although I felt close to many students and lived with them, ate with them, and went to their classes and parties, I spent my time almost exclusively with the white students. There were about 30 black students (10% of the student body). They sat at one long table in a corner of the cafeteria and had their own caucus. In my 6 months of daily contact with students at the seminary, I never went over to their table, never attended a caucus meeting (although

I occasionally attended the women's caucus meetings), and never sat in on the courses largely attended by black students.

I did not see the part that I, a white person, played in reproducing the distance between the black and white students at the seminary. But I did analyze how other white students maintained segregation. I argued that faculty and administrators taught the white students to believe that community could be achieved without interacting with those unlike them. As a white female student put it to her friends, "I feel community with the blacks even though they have their own caucus and sit at their table. I don't actually have to commune with them to experience community with them" (Kleinman, 1984, p. 77). Thus the white students could refrain from interacting with the black students and still feel they were good liberals.

My book explored how seminarians were encouraged to embrace a demystified role. At this seminary, students were taught to reject an authoritative professional role as elitist and to develop personal and egalitarian relations with those they would eventually serve. I wrote a separate chapter in which I argued that the women had some ambivalence about this ideology because they felt that parishioners would challenge their claim to the ministerial role. Although the women felt an affinity for the personalized, peerlike role, they did not feel they could realistically embrace it. My analysis put the women in a positive light because it suggested that they wanted to live out humanistic values but were denied the opportunity to do so.

What about the black students? The few data I had indicated that at least some of the black students questioned the humanistic ideology. I now sense that they wanted their education to give them unique skills and knowledge and the authority that went with the claim to professional expertise. In retrospect, I feared exposing them as careerists or elitists because I, like most of the white students, appreciated the humanistic ideology. I did not see that my fear of exposing the blacks as having different reactions from the whites kept me from interacting with them and finding out if my hypothesis was correct. Worse, I did not indicate the race of students when I quoted them in my book. I listed the gender of the student and his or her year in the program. At the time, I thought that homogenizing the whites and the blacks meant that I was being fair. The following example is taken from my book (Kleinman, 1984). A seminar is in progress. The student who breaks the norm is black and the others are white. The black student said,

"Last summer I was driving a bus and, from listening to people and talking to people, I sensed that people are hungry for community. I think it's a good time to be a minister." Everyone nodded. Another student said, "And this ministering may even happen while driving a bus." The first student said, "Hey, wait, I don't want to drive a bus. I'm not so sure ministering goes on there." The second student said, "Sure it does. You can minister while driving a bus!" The six others in the seminar agreed with the second student and criticized the first one rather strongly for sounding elitist. (p. 46)

Such incidents gave me twinges, although I tried to ignore them. At the time I believed that having the hypothesis that black students felt negatively about the egalitarian ideology meant that I was racist. If the white students had rejected the ideology and the black students had accepted it I am quite sure that I would have pursued the matter. I felt fine about portraying the white students as self-interested.

My unexamined fears led me to leave out what I now see as an important part of the story. Perhaps I was right that the black students did not take to the humanistic ideology, which in turn would have raised the question, Why? I think the seminary offered blacks one of the few traditional routes to a decent living and some prestige. The preacher has a valued role in many black communities. Unlike the more privileged white male students, the black students could not take their seminary education for granted. The white male students could afford to adopt the generous position of the egalitarian minister (at least while still in the seminary). Perhaps the black students, even more than the white women, could not.

My white liberal ideology, then, kept me from gathering data (or examining the data I had) that might portray the black students as less than perfect humanitarians. Was I only trying to protect the black students? No. I also protected my liberal self-image. Failing to examine the black students' perspective(s), I wrote a story that was incomplete and less complex than it might have been. Not one reviewer of my book commented on the relative invisibility of the black students in the story. I surmise that the white (probably liberal) reviewers felt as I did, that treating black and white students' experiences as synonymous (and positive) indicated an enlightened, nonracist view. My personal ideology, then, fit well with the theories of the time. Today's social scientists are more likely to challenge studies that equate the beliefs of blacks and whites.

But Jennifer Hunt (1989) also found herself avoiding the topic of race in her study of city police: "The fact that my fieldnotes demonstrate a relative absence of material on race, despite the abundance of data available, does suggest that I cultivated a blindness to manage my own discomfort with the issue" (p. 67).

We must consider who we are and what we believe when we do fieldwork. Otherwise we might not see how we shape the story. Perhaps later, once we are involved in our next project, we will recognize gaps in our earlier analyses that resulted from our tightly held views. We do ourselves a favor if we reflect on these matters while we are in the field.

CONSTRUCTING OBJECTIVE ACCOUNTS

As the preceding example illustrates, fieldwork analyses reflect our identities, ideologies, and political views. Yet we often omit them from our published accounts because we want to present ourselves as social *scientists*: objective and neutral observers (Gusfield, 1976; Hunter, 1990; Van Maanen, 1988). As Mary Louise Pratt (1986) noted,

> Fieldwork produces a kind of authority that is anchored to a large extent in subjective, sensuous experience. . . . But the professional text to result from such an encounter is supposed to conform to the norms of a scientific discourse whose authority resides in the absolute effacement of the speaking and experiencing subject. (p. 32)

Along with mainstream sociologists, fieldworkers regard sympathetic accounts with suspicion. Does our sympathetic tone mean that we were "sucked into" participants' perspective? Barbara Katz Rothman (1986) suggested that sociologists criticize fieldworkers who display too much sympathy for those they study. She wrote about women who faced the painful choice of aborting their fetuses after amniocentesis revealed a birth defect:

> It is a real bind. If I stick to the neat hypotheses, the simple objective level of analysis, I don't get at the fundamental issue, the core of the experience women face when they use amniocentesis. But when I share the horror at the core, I risk being dismissed as not only not scholarly or sociological, but just plain hysterical, overemotional. The same way the women's grief is dismissed as "hysterical." (Rothman, 1986, p. 53)

Omitting sympathy from written accounts contradicts the rule that fieldworkers should sympathize with those they study during their research and then get the insider's view of participants. But we communicate our insider's view in particular ways. As Howard Becker (1970a) pointed out, we usually write about cynicism rather than idealism among those we study. Although taking a cynical stance represents an emotional inclination, fieldworkers equate cynicism with the absence of emotion. We equate cynical accounts with objectivity because they lack emotional language.

Jeffrey Goldfarb (1991) defined cynicism as "a form of legitimation through disbelief" (p. 1). When we write a sociological analysis, we do not want to give readers the commonsense story they already know or just feed them what participants told us. To win credibility from our readers, we want to convince them that we did not accept participants' "sad tales" at face value. Erving Goffman's (1961) concept of sad tales cynically indicates that these are merely stories rather than real troubles that befall participants.

Readers tend to expect a sympathetic account of the life of the under-dog. But, even in that case, readers expect to learn that appearances are deceptive. We typically write the following story: Despite the bad circum-stances participants find themselves in, they manage to work the system or set up an alternative. Given the political leanings of most fieldworkers, we are unlikely to write a story that presents the TV version of poverty: "they ain't got money, but they got love." We prefer to portray participants as gritty, savvy, and streetwise, responding in creative ways to bad situations.

Because we assume that readers already side with those we studied (the underdogs), we expect them to interpret deviance among participants (such as lying, stealing, and so on) as creative strategies rather than as immoral acts. For example, we learn that the homeless place large orders for food to be delivered to nearby addresses, with the intent of retrieving the food from the trash after no one comes for it (Hill & Stamey, 1990). In the context of the article, we may even applaud such acts. These portrayals ensure that we do not think of participants as passive victims, as those who suffer in silence or, worse yet, complain. Whether poor (Stack, 1974) or mentally ill (Goffman, 1961), they are active players, finding their way through a thicket of difficulties. But the taboo against portraying participants as victims may also lead us to omit a central feature of their experience—the physical, emotional, and psychological pain of living under harsh material conditions.

For example, in Ronald Hill and Mark Stamey's (1990) study of the homeless, we learn about "acquiring possessions" (p. 307), "income sources"

(p. 308), and "types of possessions" (p. 311). This neutral, seemingly objective language suggests that the homeless have no special problems; they practice "consumer behaviors" like the rest of us. We learn how homeless people create a sense of home despite their limited possessions. We appreciate the authors' attention to the homeless's creative acts and hard work. We are convinced that the homeless try to build the sense of pride that middle-class people often obtain from home ownership and other possessions. But we wonder whether these attempts are as restorative as the authors suggest. Elevating the status of the homeless by applying largely middle-class terms to them also trivializes their pain. To some extent the authors are aware of what their account leaves out:

> This perspective on the homeless does not imply that they are without need. Many go hungry frequently and find themselves without shelter on a regular basis. Further, the most needy—the mentally ill and the physically disabled—are the least likely to be able to devise and employ the survival strategies described. (Hill & Stamey, 1990, p. 320)

Thus normalizing accounts may restore dignity to participants but then romanticize them. In the mid-1970s, when I (Sherryl) was an undergraduate at McGill University, we read Erving's Goffman's (1961) *Asylums* for a graduate seminar in deviance and social control. Most of us were taken with the book and its demystification of the deviant. Mental patients were, we learned, just like everyone else. The faculty member who taught the course, Prudence Rains, asked if we thought the book romanticized life in a mental institution. We were perplexed: Who would think that life in a total institution was fun after reading Goffman's account?

I think Rains meant that Goffman's tale omitted what it feels like to have experiences that make you think you are crazy. As Gary Alan Fine and Daniel Martin (1990) explained,

> To Goffman, the goal [in *Asylums*] is to discover how the world is "subjectively experienced" by the patient. To the reader, the book represents anything but. The essays represent how a "sane" Goffman would *himself* experience a large mental hospital if he was incarcerated against his will. Readers learn precious little about how patients experience their own world or, at the least, how they report this experience. Only rarely does one gain a sense that these are people whose behavior was seen as sufficiently strange ("dysfunctional") that they belonged at St. Elizabeth's. (p. 93)

Goffman's account convinces us that mental institutions are terrible places that would worsen *anyone's* mental state. But by normalizing the inmates, it became difficult for researchers to focus on mental patients' disturbing experiences (but see Estroff, 1981). Perhaps researchers hesitate to describe deviants' behaviors or beliefs as bizarre, fearing others will accuse them of bias or naivete. Similarly, sociologists ignored one of D. L. Rosenhan's (1988) findings, namely, that patients (not the physicians) in mental institutions could detect that the researchers admitted as "patients" were fraudulent.

Yet objectivist accounts may persuade us precisely because of the omission of participants' pain. John Van Maanen wrote in a letter to us, "Certainly it is possible that *Asylums* is a powerful book *because* of its objectivist stance and would have been less moving had [Goffman] tried to include 'mental states.' " Gary Alan Fine and Daniel Martin (1990) argued that *Asylums* can be read as satire: "Like much satire, the most absurd or outrageous events are depicted in a deliberately unremarkable style" (p. 105). By believing that Goffman gave the facts rather than took a side, some readers became more convinced that mental institutions are unfit for humans. Thus some researchers may use the realist rhetoric to create powerful social criticism (Rosaldo, 1989).

Focusing exclusively on others' pain can also romanticize them. We might portray participants as victims but treat them as heroes *by virtue of* their victimization. Such accounts would likely omit participants' angry demeanor or nasty behaviors.

In addition to excluding pain, field studies often fail to take seriously the joyful feelings of those we study. As Mary Jo Neitz and James Spickard (1990) pointed out, most sociologists of religion omit the experience of the divine in people's everyday lives. Taking religious experiences seriously might make researchers look like they were taken in by participants and did not have adequate analytic distance. But, by avoiding such experiences, we fail to learn how people manage to weave a sense of the sacred into the mundane activities of their lives.

SNEAKING EMOTIONS THROUGH THE BACK DOOR

There is one place where fieldworkers break the taboos of scientific writing: in their confessionals about methodological adventures (Van Maanen, 1988) and in the appendixes of their ethnographies. But we are careful about when and where we publish our confessionals. We tend to write them when the professional coast is clear; that is, when we are less vulnerable to others' criticisms. By placing these pieces in an appendix, we suggest that the information to be found there is merely a supplement to the real story. Or we put our confessionals in edited collections on the personal side of fieldwork (e.g., DeVita, 1990; Shaffir & Stebbins, 1991; Whitehead & Conaway, 1986). In both forms we safely quarantine the confessional from the substantive story. This has a rhetorical effect: The separation implies that our objective analysis is untainted by any troubling (subjective) experiences we had during data collection. Readers can then trust our substantive tale and feel warmed by our confessional.

Others' confessionals can help us with our own research problems. However, confessionals are usually success stories. Susan Krieger (1991), a sociologist who is known for writing risky, self-disclosing material, discovered that she too had written a success story:

> I was troubled by a sense that the smoothness of my tale was partly false. . . . What if, instead, I had produced a less justified personal account that was full of more uncomfortable and unresolved feelings? . . . [W]hen it came to my own background story, experimentation did not seem in order. My personal feelings seemed to need to be structured in a form that was traditional and clear cut (a success story), or else they would be viewed as self-indulgent, irrelevant, unpublishable. (p. 50)

As in (male) mythological tales, the researcher becomes the hero who went on a dangerous journey and lived to tell us about it. The author can admit that she or he did not follow the logical, linear path of the substantive account, but confessionals still say "Here's how I got from there to here," with "here" being a separately published, polished account. Although authors do not refer to the published story as *the* story, and many sociologists would think such a view naive (Davis, 1974), success stories communicate that idea. Given current professional standards, we shy away from providing accounts that say "Here are the multiple ways that things could be interpreted," or "Here's how I got to this provisional story."

Success implies that the author transcended any troubling feelings, at least by the time the account was written. Additionally, published confessionals represent success through a "selection bias" because editors of collections usually ask successful authors to write about any problems they faced during their careers. Rarely do we read an account of a failed project (but see Riesman & Watson, 1967).

Ironically, confessionals can legitimate our realist tales, just as published, substantive tales free us to confess our methodological sins. Confessionals prove to fellow fieldworkers that we were really there. We were not cold scientists but vulnerable humans who suffered, had doubts, and made mistakes. Without such experiences, others might wonder if we had the emotional capacity to get close enough to participants to understand them. Hence our carefully placed confessionals—of the second-worst things that happened to us (Lofland & Lofland, 1984)—allow us to prove our human credentials (Berger, 1981) without tainting our claim to objectivity.

3. IMMERSION VS. ANALYTIC IDEALS

We expect fieldwork to absorb us and provide a sense of "gaminess and adventurous zest" (Johnson, 1975, p. 3). We relish the lived experience of field research, freed from our otherwise desk-bound existence. The adventure, we believe, comes from immersing ourselves in a group or setting, spending as much time as possible, in as many situations as possible, with the people we study.

Most sociologists' ideal fieldworker is the anthropologist. We think of anthropologists as those who get fully immersed: They spend a year or two in an exotic place, get to know the community, and write notes on what they have observed, heard, and experienced. Then they return home and analyze their data. Even though most sociologists do not know what anthropologists actually do, we measure our performance against this ideal.

But field researchers have been taught another ideal: to interweave analysis with data collection. Analysis presumably begins when we start the project and continues well after we have stopped collecting data (Lofland & Lofland, 1984). Many researchers promote this ideal when they ritualistically cite Barney Glaser and Anselm Strauss's (1967) grounded theory approach in the methods section of their accounts.

Most field researchers value both immersion and analytic engagement, but we suspect that many practice the first and put off the second until data collection ends. Although most of us write voluminous fieldnotes on all that happens, how many of us write *interpretations* (for example, in our notes on notes) of what we saw and heard? We suspect that fieldworkers often elude one of the central "oughts" of qualitative research: to simultaneously collect data and analyze it sociologically.

Acting Like Scientists

Although scholarly reputations ultimately rest on publications, field-workers anchor their identity to immersion and data collection. We trust others' analyses if we believe that their notes describe their observations instead of their subjective states. But this objectivist view of fieldnotes has costs. Those who hold this view may worry about slanting their findings and thus refrain from recording their thoughts and feelings. By censoring their notes, fieldworkers may believe that they can prevent their views from contaminating the research: They did not just see what they wanted to see. We especially distrust our early reactions in the field, expecting them to be misinformed, flawed, or stereotypical. As good field-workers, we trust only the long-term knowledge we gain in the field. But, if we avoid writing about our reactions, we cannot examine them.

We cannot achieve immersion without bringing our subjectivity into play. But we convince ourselves that we can get close to participants exclusively as researchers. Thus we get two kinds of legitimacy. First, we immerse ourselves in the setting and feel like real fieldworkers. Second, we downplay our reactions and feel like good social scientists.

From there, we collect masses of data: We write detailed notes on who said what to whom, who did what, and what happened next. Accumulating a thick data set soothes fieldworkers' fears about the legitimacy of quali-tative research. By leaving out analytic commentary (especially when it is emotional), the data take on an obdurate quality. The notes become recorded facts rather than constructed understandings. If anyone ques-tions what we found, we can point to our thick folders of notes on "what happened." The fat data set validates fieldworkers and their research in the same way a large N legitimates quantitative work. By omitting our analytic thoughts and feelings from note taking, we come to believe, like positivists, that data collection and analysis are distinct stages of research.

Maintaining "Continuous Coverage"

Fieldworkers measure their competence by degrees of immersion. If field researchers cannot produce proof of immersion, they lose their readers' trust. Consequently, when fieldworkers talk to each other about their projects, a familiar question comes up: "How often do you go to the field?" Their legitimacy depends on how much time they spend there. For example, I (Sherryl) had an encompassing fieldwork experience in graduate school.

I lived in a seminary dorm for 6 months and spent almost all of my time with ministry students. Qualitative and quantitative researchers were impressed with my around-the-clock field experience. Field researchers came to accept me as one of them; the fieldwork experience served as a rite of passage into their community. In job interviews and in my first job, I found that others treated my research experience as a sign of commitment to sociology.

For my next project, I studied an alternative health center, where I attended meetings, retreats, parties, and other events and conducted lengthy interviews with key participants. This limited involvement (compared to my first major study) made me feel I was shirking my responsibilities. I felt I could not understand the Wholeness Center as well as I had understood Midwest Seminary, even though my level of involvement was probably typical of field studies. Most field researchers in sociology cannot live in the settings they study and spend intermittent time in the field. John Lofland and Lyn Lofland (1984) suggested that field studies are often based on conversations and interviews rather than on observations.

Yet the anthropological ideal continues to haunt some of us. We find ourselves oriented to the next field visit and the next interview rather than the one that just occurred. It is as if we are only as good as our *next* field effort. "Being there" offers a sense of omnipotent authority (Van Maanen, 1988): We feel better when we say, "I spent 20 hours in the field this week" than "I spent 20 hours making sense of the data that I collected last week."

Compulsive Data Collection

Fieldworkers know that they must do more than maintain continuous coverage in the field. We have to provide written proof of our visits. Because our credibility depends on recording what we see and hear, we may become obsessive about writing fieldnotes:

> Once you have established a regime of jotting regularly and then making disciplined, full notes, it can come to have a demand and a logic of its own. You can come to feel that unless something you remember appears in your full notes, you are in peril of losing it. That is, you come to experience a *compulsion* to write up everything lest it be lost forever. (Lofland & Lofland, 1984, pp. 67-68)

Both of us have experienced this compulsion and how good it felt to be compulsive about writing notes. Typing our notes to the point of exhaustion felt satisfying. As one of the anthropologists Jean Jackson interviewed (1990b) explained, "I think there was something about the typing of the notes that was very important . . . a ritual. That part of the day when you felt you were accomplishing something" (p. 18). Participating in this ritual tells us that we are serious, committed fieldworkers. John Lofland and Lyn Lofland (1984) suggested a similar outcome. After discussing the compulsion to take notes, they wrote that "upon reaching that level of felt responsibility for logging data, you are fully engaged in fieldwork" (p. 68). Fieldnotes, then, become a professional badge. As another anthropologist told Jean Jackson (1990b), "Fieldnotes is an extension of that rite of passage called fieldwork. That says it . . . fieldnotes becomes one of those objects that bring good out of this rite of passage" (p. 12).

Justifying Analysis Avoidance

For some fieldworkers, feverish note taking accompanies an equally fierce omission of their feelings and analytical thoughts. We may become obsessive about writing notes in order to escape from our feelings. John Johnson (1975) hinted at this avoidance: "Upon coming home again, I recorded fieldnotes for *seven hours*. In retrospect, that also appears to be a reflection of my feelings of anxiety, apprehension, worries about doing a good job, and the like" (p. 152). Compulsively engaging in what John Johnson (1975) later called his "demented recording ritual" (p. 152) relieves anxieties and makes fieldworkers feel productive.

When we omit our analytical material and our feelings, we probably also leave out details of the events that provoked strong emotional reactions in us. For example, Simon Ottenberg (1990) recalled,

> I remember many things, and some I include when I write even though I cannot find them in my fieldnotes. . . . I remember a great deal of haggling over payments for information, but my notes reveal little of this or of the anger that it brought me. Nor do my notes reflect the depression occasioned by my linguistic failures. (p. 144)

At the time, fieldworkers probably think of their actions as assiduous labor rather than avoidance behavior. They feel justified, even virtuous, about recording analytically barren notes. As a colleague noted,

> This ratio of roughly one day out of the field for every two in the field did not provide enough time to thoroughly analyze the material as it was being

collected. While I considered setting aside more days to analyze the material, I felt it more important to obtain the total immersion in the field and leave some of the sorting out for the write-up phase.

And Martha wrote in a memo to Sherryl,

> Why did I put off analyzing my fieldnotes? I felt overwhelmed by my data. I felt I'd accomplished something just to write down every shred of data I could remember. I felt I needed a reward of "time off" mentally after getting data "logged." So I didn't have the concept at the time that I was taking time away from analysis. I just didn't have enough time for it. Does that make sense to you? I felt that it was something that I could make up for later, and I viewed my data as something ephemeral I couldn't let get away. I wish I had felt the same way about analytical efforts, and treated time analyzing the data as something ephemeral and precious in its own right. (February 1992)

It is unfortunate that some of us worry about losing data but not our thoughts about the data. If we believed in the premises of sociology—that interaction is patterned, that people share meanings, beliefs, and behaviors—then we would trust that the patterns we missed while we were writing will still be there when we return to the field. We are *more* likely to forget our insights into what we observed. Some of us later regret that we did not write them down:

> I did not keep a diary and only occasionally incorporated diary-type material into my fieldnotes, a fact that I very much regret today. But we were brought up in a positivistic age where personal impressions were seen as less important than the "facts out there," which had a sense of reality that some anthropologists find misleading today. Since I do not have a diary to jog my memory of personal experience, my fieldnotes seem distressingly "objective." This is, of course, an illusion. (Ottenberg, 1990, p. 144)

As Simon Ottenberg later learned, "raw" notes do not exist. Each time we describe events, people, and their exchanges, we know our words implicitly judge what we have observed and heard. Because our "headnotes" (Ottenberg, 1990, p. 144), or unwritten memories of events, still govern what we see, we should put them down on paper where we can examine them:

> My written notes repressed important aspects of field research. But my headnotes are also subject to distortion, forgetting, elaboration, and I have

developed stereotypes of the people I study as a consequence of using this mental material over the years. (Ottenberg, 1990, p. 144)

Cutting Corners

Fieldworkers, we have suggested, are conscientious about writing fieldnotes (partly for the reasons we have discussed), but we suspect that they are not as committed to transcribing tape-recorded interviews. Those who have transcribed tapes know how difficult and time-consuming it is. Although one can be driven about anything, it is more difficult to sustain that attitude toward transcribing than toward typing notes. You have to keep stopping the tape rather than moving on.

What do we do? Several researchers have confessed to us that they let tapes of in-depth interviews pile up and do the next interview before listening to or transcribing the previous tape. Others may try to reach a compromise with their stockpile of tapes. As one researcher told us, "I'm just transcribing the interesting interviews. I'm jotting down notes on the others." We do not know how typical this practice is. But even fieldworkers who transcribe fully may fail to regard their interviews as field data. Do we write about how we chose who to interview, what transpired in setting up the interview, and the sights and sounds surrounding the interview? Fieldworkers may neglect contextual information when it comes to interviews.

What other practices have consequences for analysis? After spending a good deal of time in the field we tire of writing "everything" down and decide it is time to pick a focus. That is not necessarily bad. However, when we cut corners because "it's time," we must recognize that this practical decision is also a *theoretical* choice. Concentrating on one part of the setting rather than on several or talking to particular participants rather than to others might be fine decisions. But know that these choices contain assumptions about what has sociological importance. Let us remember to ask ourselves, "Why is this pattern of interaction or subgroup more interesting than others?" Even when we select data deliberately, we might later regret omitting the details of those "uninteresting" interactions. They provide useful comparisons to the "interesting" events or shed light on them.

Taming the Data Set

Nearing the end of data collection, fieldworkers' anxiety about whether they will know how to make sense of the data increases. Suddenly, those fat file folders that assuaged our fears about the subjectivity of field research become a huge monster that we feel incapable of taming. Kurt Wolff (quoted in Johnson, 1975) wrote of "the fear that I should be overwhelmed by the mass of my notes; I could not possibly keep in mind all the veins, lodes, and outcroppings of that growing mountain of typescript" (pp. 148-149). Jean Jackson (1990a) suggested that anthropologists' fear of losing their notes ironically represents a secret desire to get rid of this burden:

> Anxiety about loss of fieldnotes has come up so many times and so dramatically—images of burning appear quite often—that I have concluded that for some interviewees fear about loss is accompanied by an unexamined attraction to the idea. The many legends, apocryphal or not, about lost fieldnotes probably fits into this category of horrific and yet delicious, forbidden fantasy. One interviewee said, "So maybe the people who lost their notes are better off." (p. 20)

Because fieldworkers know that their written products—theses, dissertations, articles, and books—are the basis of their reputations, the fear of analysis may become paralyzing. Some field researchers get so anxious that they put aside their project for a long time or abandon it altogether. Even the thought of rereading our notes may be intimidating; some of us dread the discovery that we have lots of pages but little understanding. We call this reader's block.

Our uneasy feelings about how to analyze the data make it tempting to take a positivistic approach to the analysis. For example, coding is one way we bring ourselves to face the data. We create categories and write statements in the margins or on separate sheets. Coding suggests that we cannot write an integrated story unless we examine the parts of the whole. But our own experiences and those of graduate students we have taught suggest that coding can become a crutch that keeps us from thinking in a holistic way about the data. Yet it can make us feel better because it allows us to believe that we know what we are doing.

Novices who use text analysis computer software find compulsive coding irresistible. Coding and computer programs legitimate what otherwise seems an unmanageable, messy, and arbitrary process. For some, learning new computer programs becomes a fritter (Nash, 1990). For others, simply *having* a computer program for text analysis eases fears about analysis. But this can cause problems. As Marilyn Tallerico (1991) found, "Novices and mentors alike occasionally resort to hyperbole, claiming that the use of computer technology added rigor, enhanced the validity, or somehow increased the respectability or value of the research" (p. 283).

Text analysis programs can help, especially as "tireless filers" (Becker, Gordon, & LeBailly, 1984). They save us the time and energy of cutting and pasting and making photocopies of pieces of data for multiple files. But we see a danger in overcoding. Students may mistakenly think that codes, like variables, merely need to be correlated to be understood:

> [T]here is the potential for a false sense of accomplishment and productivity to be engendered by the ability to quickly and efficiently code, sort, search, and organize the data base. Although undeniably convenient, the facilitation of such tasks must be recognized as the most perfunctory aspect of data analysis and certainly in no way approaching the importance of interpretive and conceptual functions. (Tallerico, 1991, p. 281)

Instead of focusing on complex themes and processes, they may use codes to create a written product that reads more like a list of findings than an integrated story.

Writing

Why do we struggle more to write about our data than to record our fieldnotes? Our problems do not stem from implicit differences between drafts of papers and fieldnotes. Rather they arise from our erroneous and costly view of note writing. Writing fieldnotes may tax us physically and mentally, yet many of us call it mindless work. Some fieldworkers say they become like a camera or video recorder to write up their notes. Writing analytic drafts, on the other hand, means that now we have to think. And we expect to write several drafts, not knowing which one will be good enough to submit to a journal.

The open-ended nature of draft writing makes it scary. But we fool ourselves if we think of analytic writing as open-ended and fieldnotes as closed-ended. Our compiled fieldnotes are hardly final drafts of what went on in the setting or group. We could add more descriptive material (which we sometimes do), but also we could add analytic material as we move along. And our unrecorded memories or headnotes dispute the notion that fieldnotes can ever be complete.

Will we feel anxious if we recognize the first-draft nature of note writing and thus the incompleteness of our data? Believing that fieldnotes are a containable, objective unit also makes us anxious, but later in the process. If we accepted that all note writing is sense-making, whether or not we explicitly write our judgments in our notes, we might feel more comfortable working analytically all along. Doing so would give us more time to figure out our story and thus would make analysis less formidable.

Note writing and analytic writing may produce opposite reactions in us because we envision different audiences for each product. When most of us write our fieldnotes, we do not expect anyone to read them. We create our notes in utmost privacy. Because no one sees our product or our process, no one can criticize the contents. Consequently, we feel free to write what we want, any way that we want. All that changes when we write analytically. Disturbing images of future audiences—our colleagues, our friends, our critics, and those we have studied—loom before us. We wonder, Do we have the right story? Can we communicate it? What will others think of it?

Our difficulties with writing are compounded by our feeling rules: We expect to be unemotional (professional) as we write. Perhaps we allow ourselves some mild excitement as we develop insights, but our feelings about the study (and especially about participants) should not interfere with our analysis. Paradoxically, the good feelings we expect to have toward participants during data collection (see chapter 4) must now turn to stone as we write our analysis. We think our physical distance from the field will foster analytic distance and thus help us produce an "objective" analysis. We also expect to feel confident about our work. We are, after all, the experts. Hence fieldworkers, like other professionals, learn that it is inappropriate to complain about our writing problems. If we admit our insecurities, some of our colleagues might think we are incompetent.

Can we work in ways that make us feel comfortable and help us produce the best work? Yes. By writing analytic notes we ultimately save time. Analytic notes are minidrafts that we can use as a basis for later drafts (see appendix). Staying in the habit of analyzing the data as we go along might also free us from such problems as writer's block or reader's block because we will continue the process of analysis rather than face a new, alien task. We will not see our efforts, once we have collected the last piece of data, as qualitatively different from what we have done all along. Hence taking the process approach from start to finish may actually shorten, rather than lengthen, the project. And, throughout our research, we are likely to feel better about ourselves and our written products.

4. FEELINGS ABOUT PARTICIPANTS

Detached Concern?

Most fieldworkers expect to develop close ties to those they study but also retain some distance. As Martyn Hammersley and Paul Atkinson (1983) noted, "There must always remain some part held back, some social and intellectual 'distance.' For it is in the 'space' created by this distance that the analytic work of the ethnographer gets done" (p. 102). But fieldworkers probably concern themselves more with closeness than with distance (Pollner & Emerson, 1983). As we stated in chapter 3, field researchers believe that they can analyze their data later, after leaving the field.

Favoring intimacy over analysis also reflects the value we place on empathy, understanding the perspective of those we study through role taking. As Herbert Blumer (1969) taught us,

> To try and catch the interpretative process by remaining aloof as a so-called "objective" observer and refusing to take the role of the acting unit is to risk the worst kind of subjectivism—the objective observer is likely to fill in the process of interpretation with his own surmises in place of catching the process as it occurs in the experience of the acting unit which uses it. (p. 86)

How do fieldworkers interpret Blumer's dictum to take the role of the "acting unit"? Blumer's words have a *cognitive* ring: We imaginatively reconstruct how participants think and feel. But fieldworkers share *feeling* rules about empathy. Some fieldworkers believe that they should feel what participants feel. Erving Goffman (1989) argued that fieldworkers can only achieve that state by repeatedly putting themselves in the same situations as participants:

> [T]he standard technique is to try to subject yourself, hopefully, to their life circumstances, which means that although, in fact, you can leave at any time, you act as if you can't and you try to accept all of the desirable and undesirable things that are a feature of their life. . . . [Y]ou are in a position to note their gestural, visual, bodily response to what's going on around them and you're empathetic enough—because you've been taking the same crap they've been taking—to sense what it is that they're responding to. (pp. 125-126)

Thus researchers who become "complete members" (Adler & Adler, 1987) in the setting will get angry when participants feel threatened, feel hurt when they suffer losses, and experience joy when they get good news.

Other fieldworkers want less involvement. But, if we do not feel what participants feel, we expect at least to feel *for* them. This feeling rule comes closest to what Candace Clark (1987) called "sympathy sentiment" (p. 295): feeling the other's emotion or feeling *for* the other's emotion. Because most field researchers call this empathy, we will use that term.

Intimate relationships usually evoke wide-ranging emotions, from sympathy to hatred. But, in our close relations with participants, we only expect good will. When we break the feeling rule by failing to have those good feelings, we may accuse ourselves of empathic incompetence. If we understood participants better, we tell ourselves, surely we would like them.

We expect to establish rapport quickly and close ties soon after. Granted, we give ourselves some time to fret about whether participants will allow us into their world (Geer, 1967). Initially, we keep a low profile, acting emotionally flat, passive, and nonthreatening, and learn enough to avoid embarrassing ourselves or getting kicked out of the field. Except for this guarded beginning, we expect to actively seek close relationships with participants. This suggests a two-stage model of feelings: a short period of anxiety and distance followed by (almost) instant closeness. Once we feel connected to the people we study, we think we must consistently feel good about them.

Thus, unlike other professionals whose goal is detached concern (Fox, 1979; Smith & Kleinman, 1989), fieldworkers expect to have powerful feelings. But we place conditions on ourselves. First, we want only strongly positive feelings. Second, we want to have them within an appropriate relationship, namely friendship. Most researchers feel uncomfortable about their sexual or romantic impulses, let alone acting on them. As Carol Warren (1988) found in her review of gender and fieldwork, "Even in writing about settings where sexual activity is fairly public, fieldworkers have remained silent about their own sexual participation or lack of it" (p. 31; see also Fine, 1992).

Fieldworkers who feel disgusted with participants probably try to transform their inappropriate feelings into "better" ones. Because researchers seldom admit this emotion work, we know little about it. Instead of doing emotion work, we suggest that fieldworkers become more aware of their feelings and use them as data. As Arlie Hochschild (1983) argued, we can use feelings as clues: "Feeling" is a

sense, like the sense of hearing or sight. In a general way, we experience it when bodily sensations are joined with what we see or imagine. Like the sense of hearing, emotion communicates information. . . . From feeling we discover our own viewpoint on the world. (p. 17)

What happens when fieldworkers break the feeling rules? What happens when fieldworkers break the display rules and express their negative feelings to participants? The rest of this chapter explores these questions.

Breaking the Norm of Equality

Some of us believe we cannot get close to participants unless we are their equals or subordinates. For our purposes, participants are the teachers and we are their students. Sometimes we exaggerate the student role to ensure that they continue to teach us. But many of us feel like beginners and wonder if the people we study think we are slow learners. In addition, we usually feel so grateful to participants for letting us hang around that we feel and act humble rather than superior.

We do not want participants to see us as better than they are, as more competent, successful, or smarter. Often their beliefs about our superiority stem from their notions about the world we represent, one that might be of a higher class or at least cleaner, safer, or freer. We also feel guilty about our comparative riches.

Yet having a higher-status role can sometimes work to our advantage. Ruth Horowitz's (1986) distant role in her study of Chicano gangs allowed her to get information from male participants. Members perceived her as a "lady reporter," a female who deserved respect. Consequently, they told her things they would not tell the women they hung around with. Over time, members started to think of her as a peer, a sexually available woman who could be treated as badly as their girlfriends. As she became more of a peer, she no longer had a role she could live with as a researcher:

> As a lady reporter marginal to the community, I did not have to be treated as a sexual object and was free as an independent person to spend time with men and ask questions. . . . After 15 months, their sexual teasing increased significantly; they commented about how good I looked, asked if I would go out with them. . . . A sexual identity, however, would greatly impede the research process. This [gang] culture creates strong parameters within which a female researcher would be very constrained as a community member. As the pressures increased to take a locally defined membership role, I was unable to negotiate a gender identity that would allow me to continue as a researcher. After 18 months I had to stop spending so much time with the gangs and turned to the study of other groups. (Horowitz, 1986, pp. 422-423)

Because fieldworkers typically study underdogs, we often find our-selves in a higher position despite our best intentions. For example, at the start of my (Martha's) study of a sheltered workshop for people with mental and physical disabilities, I expected to be on the side of the trainees (called "employees" in the workshop). Because the workshop hired peo-ple without disabilities on occasion, I worked part-time, alongside the employees.

But I was not one of them. From start to end they saw me as a "competent adult," a status they lacked and valued above all. The employees were curious about my adult life; they asked me about my husband, my sex life, and whether I had children. They wanted to know what I did for fun, where I traveled, and how. Answering some of their questions allowed them to know me better. But talking about my greater opportunities and valued adult roles (spouse, potential parent, car owner, driver, etc.) also accentu-ated the differences in our life-styles and may have reminded them of what they lacked. I felt guilty about that.

I felt even guiltier when employees and staff put me in the role of adult or overseer. Employees occasionally used me to resolve their conflicts and demanded my opinion on disputed matters. They asked this of staff members, but rarely of each other. Sometimes the staff asked me to check the quality of employees' work. During staff meetings, I was asked now and then to "keep an eye on things" to make sure the employees were not breaking workshop rules. On one occasion I felt conflicted but neverthe-less told an employee (who routinely stopped his work and wandered about the workshop) to sit down and work. On another, I stopped two employees from roughhousing.

At these times, I felt like a hypocrite and a babysitter. There I was, a person on the side of the employees, telling them what to do. My actions flew in the face of my desired role. I thought the workshop's structure infantilized the employees. Despite the adult-centered rhetoric of staff and supervisors, staff members often treated the employees like children.

My unease helped me understand both the employees and the staff members. The employees' resistance to my offer of equality led me to comprehend their internalized, conventional notions of adulthood. Being married and "able" put me in a different category; to them, I was a normal adult. Hence I received the deference due a competent adult, even though I was a student rather than a person with a job. They treated me as someone special and assumed I would succeed after getting my degree. The value they placed on competence exceeded any other set of values, such as how friendly, kind, or generous I was.

My feelings of guilt helped me question staff members in interviews about their feelings for the employees. I discovered that staff members also felt ambivalent about exerting authority because their ideology dictated that they (like me) should not treat the employees as children. Thus my higher status role provided data I could not have gotten from becoming more like the employees (an impossibility anyway). My position enabled me to develop empathy for staff members. Without my guilt about disciplining adult-aged people, I might have dismissed the staff members' confessions of ambivalence as rationalizations. Having been in a similar position, I believed them.

We can learn from any vantage point as long as we know what roles we occupy in different situations. Our feelings while in a particular role might mirror those who hold a similar role in the setting. For example, David Karp's (1980) uneasiness in frequenting pornography shops led him to better understand impression management problems that the regulars faced. Thus our feelings suggest hypotheses about how others, members of a subgroup in the setting or perhaps outsiders, feel about themselves and each other. If we examine our uncomfortable feelings rather than dismiss them, we can gain insights into how others feel and why.

Negative Feelings

Fieldworkers often resort to a quantitative, linear perspective when it comes to empathy. We believe there is such a thing as the right amount of empathy and we expect our good feelings to grow incrementally over time. Presumably, these good feelings will dissolve our initial confusion, fears (Sanders, 1980), and anxieties.

We suspect that field researchers continue to feel uncomfortable at least some of the time. Our feelings about those we study are situational; they depend on what participants say or do (or do not say or do). We will like them some of the time and dislike them at other times. In addition, we might feel ambivalent about them, their words, or their actions. Sometimes we experience emotions simultaneously (Ellis, 1991). Hence we do not just feel good or bad, comfortable or uncomfortable. We can, for example, feel angry *and* sad.

A dominant feeling could mask threatening emotions that the researcher would rather suppress. Claudia Koonz (1987) became aware of layers of feelings in her interviews with Nazi women:

> Boredom hovered. *Bored?* I asked myself. How can you be bored? This may be the only Nazi leader you ever meet in your lifetime. All the same, this interview seemed interminable and oddly predictable, once it had become clear that the [leading Nazi woman] had not changed at all in the years following Hitler's defeat. Boredom masks depression, and under depression, lowering rage. (pp. xxvii-xxviii)

Expecting ourselves to have one feeling (e.g., comfort or connection) in all situations is unrealistic. What do we do when we find ourselves lacking empathy or feeling negatively about participants?

TRYING TO IGNORE OUR FEELINGS

If we acknowledge our anger or disappointment with participants, we face our biggest fear: that we are unempathic and thus incompetent. It is easier to try to ignore our inappropriate feelings and drift in and out of an awareness of them. For example, when I (Sherryl) studied the Wholeness Center in the early 1980s, I expected to side with the organization and especially the volunteers and staff members, all of whom were female. I discovered inequalities in the organization and learned that the women received the fewest rewards. The women's plight inspired my sympathy, thus leaving intact my self-image as an empathic fieldworker. But the women did not seem to mind getting less pay or having less influence over organizational decisions. At times I thought of them as spineless, failing to stand up for their rights.

I was bothered by my anger and disappointment. Some days I felt my anger was justified; other days I felt angry at myself for being angry at them. I knew something was wrong and needed to figure out why I felt so uncomfortable. But I put aside my discomfort for a long time. Instead, I kept collecting data, leaving my emotions out of my fieldnotes. Because I attended meetings at the center as an observer, but not as a participant, I spent my time writing copious notes that I later typed. Doing concentrated observations and recording voluminous notes allayed my fears of incompetence.

When we ignore our uncomfortable feelings we might think we have achieved the proper emotional state for analytic distance. Feeling distant, indifferent, or numb makes us believe that we have freed ourselves from feelings and thus can be objective. Like focusing a camera to distinguish the subject from the background or tuning the radio to get rid of the static, we believe we have successfully set aside our feelings and now can see and hear better. Ironically, we use the positivist ideal of feeling little to convince ourselves that we are indeed good field researchers.

But the emotional state we value will *inhibit* analysis. Moving from anger to distance need not mean that our head now controls our heart. Distance can indicate that we are numb to our feelings. As Trudy Mills and Sherryl Kleinman (1988) pointed out, "Numbness may protect the individual from experiencing particular feelings [but] numbness itself is an *overpowering* feeling-state" (p. 1012). It involves a reduction, not an enhancement, of our cognitive faculties.

Ignoring or suppressing feelings are emotion work strategies that divert our attention from the cues that ultimately help us understand those we study. In the case of the Wholeness Center I (Sherryl) should have asked myself, What kinds of assumptions about countercultural organizations, women's mobility, and paid work am I bringing to the study? What kinds of assumptions or ideas do the participants have that differ from mine? Because we are of similar age, class, and educational background, how have we come to hold different views (if indeed we do)? Do the women feel happy about their position or are they hiding their resentment? Do they recognize differences between themselves and the (better-paid, higher-status) male practitioners? Do they think of themselves as having less? What do they want?

My anger, then distance, from the women led me to put off doing in-depth interviews with them for about a year. Thus I did not do what might (and eventually did) make it easier for me to understand their perspective on the organization. (A fuller analysis is found in the next chapter.)

Feeling distant only helps in the short run. Numbness and self-estrangement spill over into other realms of our lives (Mills & Kleinman, 1988; Smith & Kleinman, 1989). Self-estrangement is discomforting, even if we interpret it as scientific objectivity. In addition, because fieldworkers strongly believe that empathy is a must for analysis, distancing will not solve the problem. We will probably have the nagging feeling that we are not doing things right. This is good because confronting our negative feelings and our fear of incompetence can help us begin analysis.

TALKING OURSELVES INTO LIKING PARTICIPANTS

Another way we deal with negative feelings is to convince ourselves that we like the participants. Some fieldworkers go overboard, telling themselves that they are lucky to hang around such fascinating people. Arlene Daniels (1983) describes her infatuation with key informants in two of her studies:

> In both these cases, I convinced myself that these were the people I wanted as cronies. It was difficult to see how the glitter of interesting personality that surrounded these figures was a product of how much I needed them. I did not realize how I had psyched myself up to admire extravagantly in order to enjoy the advantages they offered me. . . . I did not face up to the self-serving nature of these feelings of friendship. (pp. 202-203)

Arlene Daniels was too hard on herself. Yes, such excitement probably did help her "maintain the energy, the 'gas' needed to propel [her] back into the field" (Daniels, 1983, p. 201). But the problem was not an individual one (self-interest). Instead it was a product of the belief that fieldworkers should feel close to and excited by those they study. Feminist researchers expect a " 'deep identification' that breathes life into that which is studied and into the woman doing the study" (Reinharz, 1992, p. 232). This expectation places tremendous pressure on researchers. If we talk ourselves into liking participants more than we do, we will probably be angry at ourselves later for having acted deceptively. As Arlene Daniels (1983) discovered,

> The realization that one has been manipulative in the formation of friendships . . . is discomforting. One tries to reduce this discomfort by ritual expressions of friendship that give a sense of assurance that one is not only a good researcher, but a good person. Therefore, one continues to respond to friendly gestures by respondents for a time after the spark of interest has disappeared. (p. 211)

Maurice Punch (1989) also found that the close relationships he formed with the police later led him to feel dishonest and "afflicted with doubts about deceit and fraudulence" (p. 198). Thus researchers who try to make themselves like participants sometimes suffer emotional costs.

What are the costs for analysis? By changing our negative feelings (at least for a while), we cannot use them to generate questions about the group or setting. We might blind ourselves to power relations or inequalities in the group because such discoveries would exacerbate our discomfort. As Shulamit Reinharz (1992) noted, our desire for rapport might lead us to romanticize participants or to see them in stereotypic ways.

Arlene Daniels (1983) eventually recognized this cost as she wrote drafts of her manuscript. At one point she wrote a completely sympathetic report about the upper-class women volunteers she studied, portraying them as hard workers who did not get enough respect. After getting feedback from colleagues, she revised the draft. In the final version, she acknowledged the hard work the volunteers did but also examined how their work helped maintain the status quo. These women, as Arlene Daniels (1988) put it, "ignore—or deny—any suggestion that their privileged position may be part of the problems they wish to solve" (p. xxi). Instead of shifting from sympathy to cynicism, she made her analysis more complex.

Redefining our earlier feelings of closeness with participants as self-serving could prod us to write a sympathetic report. In our eyes, participants have become not only the good people who let us study them but the authentic actors. We, on the other hand, have become the instrumental researchers who feigned friendship. Again the root of the problem is our expectations of rapport and identification.

Some researchers unabashedly feign friendship in order to build participants' trust. Jack Douglas (1976) believed that "in building affection and trust it does not matter whether the researcher is honest or merely doing presentational work. . . . But he must be convincing" (p. 136). Jack Douglas's friendships with various insiders reveal a fundamental difference in how researchers define participants. Instead of assuming that informants were honest, he and his colleagues suspected that participants opportunistically deceived, charmed, and evaded the researcher's goals.

From our perspective, defining participants as manipulators on equal footing with the researcher is an emotion work strategy. By trusting informants "never more than necessary" (Douglas, 1976, p. 133) fieldworkers use cynicism as a defense. We warn that using an approach based on distrust will work against the field researcher if participants accept his or her friendship as genuine and then learn of the deception. Moreover, any problems the researcher experiences from this subterfuge will be emotionally difficult to bring into the analysis (e.g., Rose, 1990).

A few researchers have told us that they think it is possible to like participants and dislike what they do. In those cases, we reach a sociological understanding that characterizes participants as good and likable despite their flawed behaviors. However, we offer this caution: If you jump to this conclusion in the early stages of fieldwork, make sure you are not ignoring your negative feelings. Believing we like participants makes us feel better about ourselves, so we will probably avoid examining all their unlikable characteristics. If we did, it might be harder to separate persons from their acts.

Both of the strategies we have considered thus far (i.e., ignoring our feelings and trying to transform our negative feelings into positive ones) discourage us from discussing our feelings with colleagues, friends, and others. Just as it is easier to see what is wrong with someone else's writing than with our own, it is easier to analyze other researchers' feelings about the people they studied. However, until negative feelings become an expected part of field research, fieldworkers will not openly talk about them.

AVOIDANCE

Because we expect to feel good about participants, fieldworkers recoil from studying settings or groups that make them uncomfortable. We can do this unconsciously; many unappealing groups do not come to mind. If we do think of studying such a group, we can decide against it by telling ourselves we are too prejudiced. Patricia and Peter Adler (1987) recommended that researchers "avoid studying settings where they have preexisting emotional conflicts or moral judgments" (p. 23). They give an example from their own experience:

> [W]hen we moved to Oklahoma, a Bible Belt state, we were intrigued by the fundamentalist religious and teaching institutions that are so popular in the area. Although it piqued our sociological curiosity, we knew that our preconceived biases and emotional revulsion about such groups precluded our ever studying these organizations. (p. 23)

We are not urging field researchers to seek out settings that disgust them, but avoiding these groups produces big gaps in our knowledge. In addition, we are not always aware of our preexisting emotional conflicts. What if we discover, once we have begun a study, that we feel uncomfortable with the participants? Should we leave or should we use that data to understand ourselves and the group? Because few studies fail to elicit emotional conflicts (Hunt, 1989), choosing a familiar, comfortable setting cannot guarantee peace of mind.

While we are in the setting, we need to learn which subgroups or individuals make us uncomfortable. We must ask ourselves, Who are we avoiding or ignoring in the field and why? If we do not ask, we risk losing data. For example, in his study of political campaign organizations, Louis Corsino's (1987) embarrassment "at having so coldly revealed the research motives lurking behind [his] volunteer image" (p. 283) led him to avoid some participants:

> I gravitated toward innocuous tasks such as cutting and pasting newspaper clippings in the backroom of the headquarters. This seemed like an activity that was safe and would separate me from the displeasing attitudes of campaign officials. (p. 283)

We should be wary of seeking comfort and avoiding conflict at the cost of our research. Recall from chapter 2 how Sherryl's avoidance of the black students in the seminary led to an omission in her analysis of professional socialization.

Feeling Proud of Feeling Different

Fieldworkers do not always expect to feel sympathetic toward the people they study and sometimes pride themselves on feeling different from them. In our graduate fieldwork courses, we have noticed that some students enter the field with a cynical attitude toward their group. Newcomers to fieldwork, they have not yet taken on the ideal of empathy but enter the class with the image of the field researcher as journalist or muckraker. They choose a group they think of as "Other" and feel confident as long as they *do not* share participants' viewpoints. These researchers fail to examine their negative feelings about participants because they equate their cynical attitudes with analytical detachment or objectivity. In addition, cynics tend to ignore their positive feelings about participants because they equate good feelings with a lack of objectivity.

We might also pride ourselves on feeling different from certain *subgroups* in the setting, especially those we did not expect to side with. For example, in the early stages of my (Martha's) research in the sheltered workshop, I disliked the behavioristic ideology that the staff shared, thinking of it as dehumanizing. When I entered the setting, I expected to empathize with the employees (the underdogs) and distrust the staff (the agents of social control). Hence I interpreted my distaste for the staff members' belief in behaviorism as an indicator of my analytic distance. By keeping staff members' beliefs separate from mine, I could think that I was being sociological: I did not confuse my own views of employees' behaviors with those of the staff. I was a good researcher—I knew whose side I was on. And I was a good person, rejecting behaviorism meant that I, unlike staff, treated the employees fairly.

As I indicated, I came to think of staff members' feelings and beliefs about the employees as reflecting more than behaviorism. And I developed some negative feelings about employees and some positive feelings about the staff. But my initial self-satisfied feeling of difference from the "agents of social control" kept me from raising questions I thought about much later: What was their understanding of behaviorism? Where did they learn it? Did they embrace it all the time or use it situationally? What did they think of it? Failing to examine my negative feelings about behaviorism made it hard for me to see that the staff sometimes used this ideology for positive ends. For example, believing that an employee's actions (behaviors) could be separated from his or her "true self" allowed the staff members to forgive employees for their misconduct. Much like fieldworkers who disapprove of what participants do, staff members separated person from action in order to feel good about employees whose actions disturbed them. Feeling good about our differences from others should be examined as much as feeling bad about our lack of sympathy.

Making Friends With the Enemy

Our feeling rules are not entirely consistent. We make an exception to the rule of sympathy when we study settings where participants routinely perform cruel acts, bring emotional harm to the innocent, or espouse beliefs that objectify others. In those circumstances, fieldworkers think their disgust or hatred is justified. For example, in his study of attendants in the back ward of a mental hospital, Steven Taylor (1987) wrote unapologetically: "During the several months of my study, I thought of the attendants as rather backward, sadistic people" (p. 298).

Typically, fieldworkers put themselves in these situations so that they can understand the phenomenon well enough to stop it. But developing cognitive empathy (understanding why people think, feel, and act as they do) can generate feelings of sympathy in the researcher. These feelings make the researcher uncomfortable. Diana Scully (1990) had this to say about the convicted rapists and murderers she studied: "As unlikely as it may seem, I found that it was also possible for me to develop unexpected empathy occasionally during the course of an interview" (p. 18).

Fieldworkers might believe that their occasional sympathetic feelings have some virtue; they are capable of recognizing the humanity of loathsome people. Researchers usually argue that participants' immoral acts stem from a social or structural problem rather than individual failures in moral behavior. They ask, What are the conditions that led these ordinary people to commit heinous acts? Do participants construct an image of themselves as good despite what they do? The sociological story typically presents participants "not as 'bad people' but as otherwise 'good people' in a 'bad place' " (Taylor, 1987, p. 296). Thus researchers sympathize with those who find themselves in the wrong place at the wrong time.

But these researchers face another problem: how to act with participants. What display rules (Hochschild, 1983) do they follow? Should researchers show that they disapprove of what participants say, think, or do? We suspect that most researchers believe that they should act as if they agree with those they study or at least refrain from displaying disagreement. Most fieldworkers believe that sympathetic displays help us acquire good data. But researchers might also find that they have compromised their morals. As William F. Whyte (1955) put it,

> I . . . had to learn that the fieldworker cannot afford to think only of learning to live with others in the field. He has to continue living with himself. If the participant observer finds himself engaging in behavior that he has learned to think of as immoral, then he is likely to begin to wonder what sort of person he is after all. Unless the fieldworker can carry with him a reasonably consistent picture of himself, he is likely to run into difficulties. (p. 317)

Reflecting on his study of the police, John Van Maanen (1979) concluded that his presence led the officers to exaggerate their actions. Thus researchers can become an unwitting audience for participants to display how tough they can be (Punch, 1989; Taylor, 1987; Van Maanen, 1979). Occasionally, members demand that researchers engage in morally dubious activities, as Richard Mitchell (1991) found in his study of survivalists. Members of other groups expect mild sympathy or a nonjudgmental attitude. In the study of rapists mentioned earlier, Diana Scully (1990) found that "the interviews were very fragile, easily destroyed by a careless remark or gesture" (p. 14) and "even the most hardened felon would talk . . . to an interested, supportive, nonjudgmental outsider" (p. 15).

But we do not always have to display agreement. Most of us are too timid to break this feeling rule, but we suspect that many settings do not require an acquiescent demeanor. Fortunately, some researchers have provided accounts of the rewards of dissent. Expressing disagreement helped these fieldworkers live with themselves and bettered their analyses. For example, David Gordon (1987) initially had a hard time studying a proselytizing group. Like others before him, he "experienced the most subjective distress, especially resentment that members refused to accept [him] as 'just' a researcher" (Gordon, 1987, p. 275). Later, he defended his own beliefs to participants rather than pretended to agree with them. To his surprise, group members remained comfortable with him. Discussions about religious beliefs became "good spirited affairs which [they] all enjoyed, rather than high pressure proselytizing" (Gordon, 1987, p. 276).

Empathic disagreement, as Gordon called it, aided the research rather than destroyed it. He discovered that previous researchers' initial distress, fear, discomfort, annoyance, and guilt led most of them to leave the field. Fieldworkers worry that participants will interpret disagreement as unfair criticism or rejection, and thus it will drive a wedge between them. But Gordon suggested that saying what one thinks can be an *engaging* experience and thus constitute closeness rather than distance. Similarly, Mac Marshall (1990) found that intervening in a drunken brawl did not cut him off from others:

Before I fully realized what I was doing I had a full nelson on the larger man, had pulled him off of his victim, and was trying to convince him to desist from such behavior.

Though strong enough to protect myself from harm, it occurred to me as I stood there that I had made a terrible mistake. All through graduate school my professors had emphasized the importance of not taking sides or getting involved in local political or interpersonal squabbles in the research community, lest one make enemies, close off potential sources of information, or even get thrown out of the research site. . . .

[T]his incident . . . not only *improved* my rapport (including with the man I had restrained!) but also contributed to the development of my personal reputation on Namoluk. . . . My actions that afternoon accorded closely with core Trukese values that contribute to the image of a good person: respectfulness, bravery, and the humble demonstration of nonbullying strength in thought and deed. (pp. 15-16)

Even if we try to avoid our uncomfortable feelings, *participants* in some settings force us to confront them. David Gordon's proselytizers made his status as potential convert so important that he could scarcely ignore his feelings about being put in that position. Such strong feelings make it difficult to refrain from speaking our minds for long. In Gordon's case, opening up discussions about his and group members' beliefs gave him data that he might not have acquired otherwise. The debating style of the interaction allowed Gordon to push participants to articulate their beliefs rather than gloss over various details.

In his field study of the mythopoetic men's movement, Michael Schwalbe (personal communication, December 1992) discovered that confronting some of the leaders provided data he might not have otherwise acquired:

> I was at a five-day gathering with about 120 men and some of the move-ment's best-known teachers. We were discussing the story "Faithful John," which was being told by Michael Meade. In one part of the story a young prince uses a ruse to abduct a princess. He takes her far out to sea before he tells her what's going on. The princess isn't at all upset by this. In fact, she's quite taken with the prince and they go below decks to make love. We were discussing this part of the story when James Hillman, one of the teachers, said to Meade, "Wouldn't the feminists object to this? After all, he's abducted her." Meade's response was that such an objection would be misguided, since this was just a fairy tale; it wasn't about real men and women. I was bothered by the glib dismissal of any concern for the political content of the imagery in the story, but I didn't say anything. I just kept taking notes.
>
> Then Hillman said something about the prince taking the princess below decks to make love "without her explicit verbal consent." He was alluding to date rape, and his tone implied that it was some sort of feminist fantasy. Some men picked up on the allusion right away. I heard a few mutter, "Yeah, like date rape." Others snickered. This was too much. I put down my pen, stood up, and said that I thought there was good reason to be concerned with the imagery in the story. I said that the story reflected a patriarchal point of view, since the woman was nothing more than an object of the prince's quest.
>
> My objection really heated things up. Meade insisted that the story wasn't patriarchal at all and we ended up getting into a shouting match. Hillman told me that I was interpreting the story "psychologically" rather than "my-thologically." Some men in the audience joined in to tell me I was off base. When the exchange was over I figured I'd blown it. Word of this would get back to the group I was studying (some of the local men were present) and I'd never get another interview. But much to my surprise two men ap-proached me at the next break period and said that they agreed with what

I'd said to Meade. Another man said he disagreed, but he respected the "ferocity" I displayed in making my statement. When I told another man, a guy I'd interviewed for the study, that I thought I'd botched things up with my outburst, he said "Not at all. You've got the admiration of every man here for the way you stood up to Meade." Then he hugged me. So it turned out that by losing my cool I learned some things. I learned that there were men present who did not dismiss a feminist critique of the sexist imagery in the fairy tales; that some of the men felt it was more important to give me support as an individual than to argue with me about gender politics; and that assertiveness was something these men valued more highly than I'd previously imagined.

Maurice Punch (1986) found himself embroiled in battles with the authorities of the progressive school he studied. They wanted to control the publication of his work and displayed a "paranoia over evaluation" (p. 79). But he believed that the long-term fight provided his best data. In his words, "It may well be that I have to propose the somewhat galling premise that my conflict with the sponsors is more revealing about them than the actual research findings" (Punch, 1986, p. 51).

Fieldworkers fear that expressing disapproval contaminates research; telling others what we think forces them to react to it and thus changes the setting. Yet, as the above examples suggest, challenging participants can reveal what they take for granted and thus give us a fuller understanding of the group.

In addition, our emotion work might well suppress the discomfort itself. As Peggy T. Thoits (1985) and Arlie H. Hochschild (1983) argued, we can sometimes change our feelings by changing our behavior. If we act friendly long enough, we might find ourselves feeling friendly. And because we associate friendly feelings with the empathy required of fieldworkers, we might "forget" our discomfort. But ignoring those uncomfortable feelings amounts to ignoring data.

At the very least, we must acknowledge our negative feelings to ourselves. This frees us to use those feelings as clues to analysis. For example, when Claudia Koonz (1987) began her interview study of women once active in the Nazi movement in Germany, she expected them to talk about their guilt over past deeds. Before she talked to one of the major organizers of Nazi women, Koonz (1987) thought that Scholtz-Klink "had decided to speak out to warn the world or simply to atone for her complicity" (p. xxi). But the woman she interviewed had no guilt and instead defended the Nazis' intentions. Koonz (1987) was aware of her disgust during the interview: "I poured more tea. Silence broken by rain pelting down on the roof. I repressed my only reaction: a fantasy . . . her face turning blue as hands closed tightly around her throat" (p. xxxi). Koonz used her moral indignation to generate research questions: "Where . . . had pity gone? What kind of moral hardening had enabled this paragon of womanliness not only to participate in the Nazi state, but to defend it so mindlessly four decades later?" (p. xxxii).

Similarly, Micaela di Leonardo (1987), an Italian-American woman studying Italian-Americans, used her mixed feelings about those she studied to ask questions about *their* ambivalence toward their ethnic group:

> What is interesting . . . is that I discovered on my own an absolute essential for [an] ethnographer's mental health: giving free rein to private expressions of hatred for one's informants, one's project, and oneself. . . . This discomfort rose to acute levels when I was dealing with informants I simply could not like. I fought back by cursing Italian-Americans. I began to talk with friends about "never wanting to see another WOP as long as I live" (I was talking, of course, about myself as well). . . . In the end this self-consciousness about my ambivalence about Italian-Americans resulted in some of the most exciting narratives I recorded. I began to ask individuals how they felt about different sorts of co-ethnics. People divided the group by class. . . . Many women saw gender as the dividing line. . . . And many informants made fun of accents and burlesqued stereotyped Italian-American attitudes. (pp. 17-18)

Unlike most researchers, Manda Cesara (1982) sought out interactions that would likely lead to conflicts over values:

> In my interaction with the Lenda, I wanted to and did experience . . . collisions. I wanted to confront their very otherness, to hear their viewpoint and let it challenge mine. . . . Collisions with the other's horizons make us aware of deep-seated assumptions that would otherwise have gone unnoticed. (p. 217)

Thus she felt she learned the most about the Lenda when their beliefs and practices clashed with hers. Similarly, Catherine Lutz (1988) learned the assumptions about emotions and gender in her own culture by comparing them with the Ifaluk.

Identifying With Participants

Researchers who have the opposite problem of identifying fully with participants can also feel uncomfortable. If those we study have been

victimized or are suffering physical or emotional pain, we might find ourselves feeling sad, angry, or depressed. For example, Linda Dunn (1991)
had the following experiences when she studied women whose husbands
had battered them:

> Night after night, I would go to bed and fall asleep immediately, only to
> wake in a few short hours and remain awake for the rest of the night. I
> diagnosed myself as depressed, but why? Exhausted, I made an appointment
> with my physician and obtained a prescription that would promote sleep.
> My inability to sleep diminished; however, extreme gastrointestinal upsets
> began, which necessitated numerous tests, diet changes and more medica-
> tion. . . . Conducting the interviews for this study was an emotionally drain-
> ing experience. I would often become choked with emotions during the
> tearful interviews. (pp. 390-391)

Dunn (1991) suggests that she took on the emotions and even the physical
symptoms of the women she interviewed:

> Retrospectively, I noted that the physical and emotional responses I experi-
> enced were parallel to those expressed by the subjects in my study. . . . I
> experienced anger and powerlessness, which resulted in sleep disorders and
> other somatic complaints that were similar to those voiced by the informants.
> (pp. 389-391)

Similarly, Barbara Katz Rothman (1986) found herself distraught over
her project on women who had experienced amniocentesis, especially
those who had received "bad diagnoses":

> I could not stop looking at it [the file on bad diagnoses], and I could not bear
> looking at it. Why was it so painful for me? For one thing, the women became
> so real to me; I came to know them, to care, to identify. Especially to identify.
> I had a baby at home. My second, born when I was 33—too young in 1981,
> if not now, for amniocentesis. I was so close, emotionally and physically, to
> the pregnancy experience, to the terrible, urgent intimacy of that relation-
> ship. (p. 50)

What should we make of these experiences? Did Linda Dunn (1991)
and Barbara Katz Rothman (1986) overidentify with the women they
studied? Overidentification, like "over-rapport" (Miller, 1952), implies
that there is a right amount of rapport and we need to stop when we reach

it. What matters more than our degree of identification is what we *do* with our feelings. Both Dunn and Rothman used their experiences to inform their analyses. Dunn dealt with her distress by talking to family members, colleagues, and other health professionals (she is a nurse) about her feelings. She thought about the help others gave her and compared her support system to the battered women's relationships. Her own network of support highlighted the paucity of support available to the women she studied. She came to understand then how others played a part in keeping the battered women from improving their lives.

Barbara Katz Rothman's (1986) grief mirrored the women's feelings about their aborted fetuses. Her grief led her to understand the women in ways that others, including the women's physicians and husbands, could not. As she reported,

> The research turned out quite differently than I had expected. True, the table of contents I envisioned is almost exactly what is coming to print. . . . But the heart of the work moved. The grief became the core of the project, and everything else fell in around it. Not one slim and restrained chapter, as anticipated, but the heart of the book is the women who got the bad news. I used their experience of grief and anguish for what it tells about motherhood, about pregnancy, and about a society that develops this kind of technology— and expects gratitude for it. (Rothman, 1986, p. 52)

Fieldworkers know they are not supposed to "go native." Converting to a group or working for a cause presumably distorts our sociological vision. The assumptions here, that participants never think sociologically and that sociologists who become converts or advocates thus lose that ability, are at best hypotheses. Benetta Jules-Rosette's (1975) conversion to the teachings of the apostolic church of John Maranke led her to make sense of that experience in herself and in others. The research Barrie Thorne (1983) conducted while participating in the Resistance movement during the Vietnam war resulted in analyses of the movement *and* the academic world:

> Being a fieldworker in this particular setting entailed especially sharp conflicts of consciousness. The detached comparative perspective of field- work was at great odds with the emotional urgency, sense of apocalypse, and demands for partisanship and collectivity which were central to daily life in the movement. . . . The conflicts of consciousness which I felt while doing fieldwork in the Resistance provided me with insight into the

movement world of meanings, as well as into the contrasting ways of knowing and feeling which are bound up in social research. (p. 233)

The researchers in this section did not ignore their feelings or talk themselves into becoming distant. Rather they allowed themselves to experience their feelings. More important, they made sociological sense of their experiences by thinking, talking, and writing about them.

The Costs of Feeling Good

Researchers probably feel most comfortable when they like participants and participants like them. When that happens, we tell ourselves that we have achieved rapport and the people we study will now take us into their confidence. Thus we feel competent and untroubled as fieldworkers.

When relations are smooth and we think we have achieved the right amount and kind of empathic feelings, we need to be the *most* alert about the analytical import of our feelings. Because we have been taught that sympathy sentiment is a prerequisite for fieldwork, we are unlikely to recognize our good feelings as data. We prefer to bask in our feelings of competence, believing that the good relations we have established reflect our skills at developing rapport. But there are good sociological reasons why we have smooth relationships with participants; figuring them out can aid our analysis.

For example, when I (Sherryl) began my study of the seminary (Kleinman, 1984) I noticed that the students instantly welcomed me into their world. I too felt comfortable with participants. I was relieved that they did not fit my image of the clergy as somber, religious, and bookish but instead acted like graduate students. How lucky I was to find a setting where participants wanted me around day and night and eagerly talked to me about their inner conflicts. Maybe I felt too lucky. So I began to think about why the students jumped at the opportunity to spend time with me. I eventually came up with several reasons, such as their inclusive, humanistic ideology, their understanding of sociology as psychology (they thought I could help them understand themselves), and their need to have a person on the outside legitimate them as ordinary people (rather than as religious fanatics). All of these became part of the story I told.

We must analyze our good feelings about participants and their good feelings about us. What do they think we are offering that makes us attractive to them? Do we give them the chance to say things they cannot talk about among themselves (thus indicating a norm in the setting)? Do they want our sympathy (because they think outsiders do not understand them)? Do we provide some legitimacy for the group?

Once we have established relationships of mutual liking with participants, we might find ourselves in situations where we offer sympathy before we understand what the action or event meant to the participant. By offering "instant sympathy," we believe we understand why participants did what they did, but we do not test it out by asking questions. For example, in my (Martha's) ongoing study of the sheltered workshop, an employee broke into the workshop at night to steal the keys to the workshop van with a friend, drove the van without a license, got caught, and was taken to jail. In a forlorn voice, Noel told me some of what happened and seemed sorry about what he had done. I thought what he did was stupid but dismissed it as a youthful indiscretion. Because he showed remorse, I offered support, making it clear that although I disapproved of his actions I was not going to hold that against him. We only talked about the incident for a few minutes and then our discussion was interrupted by a staff member. She snapped at Noel, telling him he had just missed his bus (we had not heard the call to board).

I liked Noel. To me he was a good-hearted soul who had made a mistake. Feeling good about Noel, I believed I understood how he felt and the sense he made of his actions. Much later I thought about the fact that he had just turned 18, the age at which such actions can have serious legal consequences. Did he know this? Was he trying to see if the staff would press charges and thus treat him like a real adult?

Because employees had few opportunities to achieve conventional adult status, perhaps this deviant action ironically offered one avenue for taking adult responsibility: getting punished by the real agents of social control (the police, the courts) rather than by the staff, who "sheltered" them. I had not asked him for the story of the event. I soon learned from the staff that they did not press charges. They tried to cover up what he had done and told him that he should not talk to others about it. They assumed that he did not know the legal significance of being 18. The staff's reaction provided important data, but instead of questioning them about it I found myself reacting the way they did: I normalized the behavior. But what reasons did *they* have for treating the event as a youthful prank that was best forgotten? Did they worry that the story might lead companies to cancel production contracts with the workshop? What were the accepted signs of adulthood to employees and to the staff?

By going along with both Noel's and the staff members' definition of the situation, I overlooked leads for analysis.

By providing instant support and failing to ask questions of our participants, we fill in our own interpretations for participants while believing we have captured theirs. To avoid this problem, we might ask, What has evoked our sympathy? Do participants see the incident in the same way? Do we share the same understanding of what has transpired or do our feelings of closeness mask different interpretations of the same event?

5. CONCLUSIONS

The seeming avoidance of values is the strongest value commitment of all, exempting one's empirical claims from rigorous self-reflection and self-criticism.

Ben Agger (1991, p. 111)

In a previous chapter, we stated that researchers should write inductive accounts of their studies, especially analyses of how their feelings helped them understand the field setting. What follows is a short version of such an account. I (Sherryl) will examine the feelings I ignored during my study of the Wholeness Center and link them to my analysis of the organization. After this account, we examine the implications of our perspective for fieldworkers' assumptions, ethnographic products, and identity. In the appendix of the book, we will discuss how fieldworkers might put their emotions into their notes.

Studying the Wholeness Center

SITUATING THE RESEARCH SELF

In the fall of 1980, I began to study a holistic health organization, just a couple of months after beginning my first academic job. I was in a tenure-track position in a prestigious, mainstream sociology department, a job that did not fit well with my self-image. I had lived through some of the ideological changes of the 1960s and 1970s and found myself, like many others of my generation, challenging the legitimacy of prestige structures and the value of formal relations.

I felt ambivalent about taking my first academic position. Did I want this rite of passage into adulthood? Now I was a professor—one who professed. I felt I should know a great deal, impress students, and publish without having to ask others for help (especially those who would later judge me for tenure). I worried that I would have to abandon the informal, egalitarian relations I valued as a student and look, talk, think, and act like an adult.

Like many of my generation, I resented these conventional, unstated (and admittedly exaggerated) expectations. So I found a setting that I hoped would allow me to keep one foot in the 1960s. In retrospect, I needed the Wholeness Center and its members to represent and live out the ideals I felt I lived out only intermittently. But despite the promising, alternative trappings of the organization, I found a disappointing (ordinary), bureau-cratic structure. One part of the Center "belonged to" private practitioners who were paid from individual clients and then paid a percentage of their earnings to the Center. The other, educational part was nonprofit, run by staff and volunteers. In dealing with the Center's financial problems, the staff rarely got paid (and received $4 an hour when they did), but the practitioners almost always got paid (about $35 an hour) for their services. This structure could hardly pass as cooperative or alternative to sociol-ogists who study nontraditional organizations (e.g., Rothschild & Whitt, 1986). Moreover, almost all of the practitioners were men and all of the staff members and volunteers were women.

As I indicated in chapter 2, I was also disappointed that the Wholeness Center was equally suspect as a conventional organization. Some of my colleagues were not convinced that the topic of an alternative organization was legitimate. Thus I felt ambivalent about the organization, a sentiment that reflected the period of the 1980s. It was a time when experiments in social change were welcomed with less enthusiasm (both within sociology and without). Yet some of us still had high hopes for alternate forms of organization that promised humanized relations.

FEELINGS ABOUT PARTICIPANTS

To the extent that I acknowledged my feelings, I felt angry at most of the participants. First, they did not seem to have a political consciousness; they mostly psychologized their problems. Second, I noticed inequalities in their arrangements that participants either did not notice or did not mind. I had mixed reactions to the staff women. I thought of their subordinate status as endemic to social relations rather than as their fault. Yet I blamed them for their silence, especially in an organization that claimed to welcome discussions of interpersonal relations. I grew uncomfortable about my negative attitude toward participants, especially the women. As a feminist and a field researcher, I felt I should have more sympathy for them. Feelings of incompetence began to plague me.

EMOTIONS AND DATA COLLECTION

As I suggested in chapter 4, I fashioned a role that allowed me to interact minimally with participants. I attended their meetings and retreats and took notes the entire time. Although I interacted informally with members before and after meetings and during parties, I became the "objective observer" the rest of the time. Participants, I discovered later, liked having a sociologist in residence; I helped legitimate the organization. I found myself typing detailed notes of who said what to whom, but I wrote little on how I felt about what I observed. I took comfort in the many pages of fieldnotes piling up on my desk.

Because I was turning my dissertation into a book and writing other articles, I compartmentalized my feelings about the Wholeness Center. Acknowledging them only on occasion, I hoped that they, like flu symptoms, would disappear soon or at least by the time I stopped collecting the data. But I felt lethargic about the project. After a while, I did not even try to psych myself up to do the field research. I thought about it as routinized work, an obligation rather than a choice. I did not want to talk about the project and concentrated instead on feeling good about my other writing. But I had a general sense of malaise and nagging feelings of incompetence.

ANALYSIS

Eventually, understanding my own ambivalence about the adult work world enabled me to appreciate the participants' dilemmas. My emotional reactions served as a mirror: I began to see that what they were doing resembled what I was doing in studying them. I wanted to do research on something different, something close to my ideological heart, but legitimate it through the conventional means of research and publication. Members of the Wholeness Center also wanted to retain certain ideals from the 1960s while gaining modern-day conventional legitimacy. They (like me) wanted the best of both worlds: to achieve conventional success while honoring the standards of their youth. Their conflicting goals began to figure prominently in the story.

Another process that facilitated analysis was that my attitudes toward the women changed once I started interviewing them. I became more forgiving as I tried to understand their perspective on the organization, how they got involved, and what they wanted from it. In their view, money was not important; they joined the organization looking for a meaningful activity that would enhance their self-esteem and provide a community of sentiment. The interviews also alerted me to the women's changing views over time; eventually they became disillusioned and believed the male practitioners took advantage of them.

In addition to the changes precipitated by interviewing, my willingness to sympathize with the women increased because of shifts in my feminist thinking. Reading Carol Gilligan's (1982) work on differences in moral reasoning between men and women and Jean Baker Miller's (1976) analysis of the value of certain traditionally feminine characteristics made me appreciate the women's actions. I began to think of the staff women as having laudable values: working for little money for a good cause.

But at some point I began to question whether inequalities actually existed in the organization. If the women wanted feelings of connection in the organization, and got them, and the men wanted a place to ply their trade, and did so, then could one speak of inequality or was the situation fair?

This equal-but-different story alleviated my worry that I was projecting my own values onto the group. Because I wanted the organization to fulfill egalitarian ideals, I wondered whether it was fair to judge them by my standards. I later gave credence to my anger, saw it as an "outlaw emotion," a " 'gut-level' awareness that we are in a situation of coercion, cruelty, injustice or danger" (Jaggar, 1989, p. 161). Members of the Wholeness Center shared an ideology of equality: each person is unique and special, equal "underneath it all." Thus they denied what I observed, namely, that members did not treat each other equally. The higher-paid, male practitioners—those looked on as the "real" professionals—controlled organizational decisions and received more respect, attention, and affection. Despite their ideology of equality, the practitioners were "more equal" than others.

As I look back, my anger served as an inequality detector. This detector, however, is fallible; we should use it to test whether or not we are witnessing an injustice. But we can only test this hypothesis if we first acknowledge such feelings as anger.

Facing my worst fear, that I was unempathic, led me to articulate my analytic position and explain why it fit the data better than some other perspective. The manuscript I am completing offers what might be called a critical appreciation of the organization. I examine members' well-intentioned attempts to live out their alternative ideals, especially in relation to their clients. But I also critique participants' methods for achieving their contradictory goal of becoming an alternative organization with conventional legitimacy. They tried to resolve this contradiction in ways that obscured the systematic inequalities in their treatment of each other.

Building Alternatives

Acting like positivists lets us feel that our work has legitimacy but fails to solve our fieldwork problems. What can we do instead? What assumptions might guide us? What will our ethnographic products look like? Will our identity as fieldworkers change?

ASSUMPTIONS

We assume that field researchers' selves and emotions are always implicated in research. We cut ourselves off from our research at a great cost to our work. As George Devereux (1967) noted,

> The behavioral scientist cannot ignore the interaction between subject and observer in the hope that, if he [or she] but pretends long enough that it does not exist, it will just quietly go away. The refusal to exploit these difficulties creatively can only lead to the gathering of less and less relevant, more and more segmental, peripheral and even trivial data, which shed almost no light on what is . . . human about man [or woman]. (p. xviii)

Thus we should discard the question "Did this researcher's feelings affect the study?" when we read fieldwork accounts and instead ask "*How* did the researcher's emotions play a part in the data collection and analysis of this group or setting?" Readers should raise this question to understand the phenomenon better rather than discredit the researcher's account.

If we incorporated the idea that emotions encompass the research process, we would begin to use all our feelings, even the ones we now consider inappropriate, as tools for analysis. We would become suspicious of solving our fieldwork problems through positivistic means. For example, if we found ourselves trying to deny our anger or hostility toward participants, we would no longer believe that our so-called indifference was an indicator of appropriate analytic distance. We would ask ourselves, Why do I feel angry, happy, or bored? Is this my only feeling? Why do I feel this way?

Our emotional reactions often reveal our political beliefs. We assume that researchers, because they are human, are also political. As Herbert Gans (1982) explained,

> [We] cannot do away with the fact that research, like all other human activities, is political; that it supports one point of view and vested interest at the expense of others. The researcher must therefore take a political stand on some issues, and he [or she] should make it clear where his [or her] sympathies lie. (p. 406)

The absence of the author's emotions in most ethnographic accounts parallels the omission of participants' emotions. In sociology and anthropology, researchers still privilege the cognitive and the behavioral over the emotional. Fieldworkers, then, ignore others' emotions as well as their own. If we believe we cannot understand a group without acknowledging our own emotions, we can hardly ignore how participants feel. In ourselves and in others, then, we should recognize and examine "desires, plans, whims, strategies, moods, goals, fantasies, intentions, impulses, purposes, visions, [and] gut feelings" (Rosaldo, 1989, p. 103).

WRITING AS PROCESS AND PRODUCT

In chapter 3, we argued that institutional time pressures may lead fieldworkers to skimp on analysis. They collect a lot of data but fail to analyze it between interviews or visits to the site. This will probably lead to writer's block or a simplified story.

But the best qualitative accounts are complex. Researchers differ in the kinds of analyses they write (see Burawoy et al., 1991; Glaser & Strauss, 1967; Lofland & Lofland, 1984), but good qualitative studies usually integrate themes rather than list them and offer contradictions and ironies rather than mundane descriptions.

Writing analytic fieldnotes will save us time in the long run. Interacting with the data set as it grows will relieve us of the anxiety we feel when we face it whole. When that time comes, we will simply continue doing what we have been doing all along: making sense of things through writing.

In addition, the process approach to writing will make our work less alienating. If we truly believed, along with Flannery O'Connor (1971), that we do not know what we mean to say until we write it down, then we might look forward to writing. If we believed that good analyses depend on understanding our feelings, then we would let loose at the keyboard. If we thought of each draft as a re-vision, then we would look forward to what the next draft brings.

Instead, we expect to know what we will write before we begin. In this view, drafts are polished versions of what we think we already know. This formulaic approach to writing only weds us to our initial ideas. We must be willing to take these ideas seriously but discard them when they no longer satisfy. Peter Elbow (1973) explained his writing process:

> I feel caught in a great swamp. The moment I try to move toward X, Y, or Z, I see that each is no good. But I can't think of any more. I keep trying them and abandoning them over and over again. . . . The problem is that I'm not taking any one of them far enough. I let myself get stopped by feelings of wrongness. . . . For I've discovered that when I force myself to take one of those paths—it doesn't much matter whether I choose X, Y, or Z—and really develop that train of thought fully towards its end, it gets me out of the swamp. I have to *force* myself to do it against that horrible feeling that it is a waste of time. And usually it is indeed wrong. But I was caught in a swamp because I didn't allow it to *be* fully X, Y, or Z. And once I do . . . then I see a whole new direction to go in that I couldn't see before. (p. 45)

Taking a process approach to writing and bringing our feelings into the analysis will change our written products. Readers would come to expect authors to present themselves as emotional agents in their accounts. Researchers would weave their feelings into the analysis rather than relegate them to the beginning or end of the story. Authors, then, would use their emotions to support—or refute—their hypotheses. In addition, readers would expect authors to disclose how their feelings about participants changed over time and how those changes reflect changes in the analysis. This would shatter two unhelpful images of the fieldworker: the perfectly empathic researcher and the perfectly distant writer. Such accounts would serve as models for future ethnographers.

Including self-reflection and emotions in ethnographic writing is not new. In the 1970s, some social scientists made their positions as authors and researchers clear. For example, John Johnson (1975) analyzed the emotional underside of his study of social workers in Child Welfare

Services and Shulamit Reinharz (1979) examined her transformation from survey researcher to experiential fieldworker.

Most researchers still try to keep themselves out of their work, believing that their method has "a life of its own," independent of themselves (Charmaz, 1990, p. 1164). But analysis is produced by our interactions with participants, even when we try to remain distant from them. Many researchers also think that their writing has a life of its own. Then we do not have to take responsibility for how we shape our stories. But, as Paul Atkinson (1992) argued, qualitative researchers should recognize the constructed nature of their fieldnotes, commentary, and ethnographic accounts. Whether we like it or not, the facts do not speak for themselves. Rather, all researchers use particular writing conventions. As Atkinson (1992) put it, "The contemporary ethnographer must make choices *in the full knowledge* of his or her textual practices, and the likely receptions on the part of readers" (p. 7, emphasis added).

This postmodern movement (Agger, 1991) within anthropology (e.g., Clifford & Marcus, 1986; Rosaldo, 1989) and to a lesser extent in sociology (e.g., Krieger, 1991; Van Maanen, 1988) has made some field researchers more aware of the constructed nature of their accounts. Margery Wolf (1992), an anthropologist, argued that feminist social scientists wrote a long time ago about issues that postmodern anthropologists now raise. Ironically, anthropologists delegitimated feminist work "for the same things the post-modernists' critiques now celebrate—like questioning objectivity, rejecting detachment, and accepting contradictory readings" (Wolf, 1992, p. 135).

Some social scientists (Douglas, 1976; Flax, 1987; Mascia-Lees, Sharpe, & Cohen, 1989; Roth, 1989) worry that fieldworkers will write accounts that substitute self-understanding for sociological understanding. Renato Rosaldo (1989) argued that there is a current "tendency for the self-absorbed Self to lose sight altogether of the culturally different Other" (p. 7). But this need not be the case. Rather, researchers could write accounts that offer understanding of the other *through* self-reflection.

Along with Margery Wolf (1992), we believe that postmodern lessons should be used to offer critical analyses of social life (see also Bourgois, 1990). But we wonder whether the move toward "the relativity of interpretation and the interpreter" (Ottenberg, 1990, p. 156) will make researchers *less* likely to write social criticism. Will researchers discount their feelings of injustice, believing that their discomfort merely mirrors personal hangups? Will female scholars, already in a less authoritative position in the social sciences than their male colleagues, gain self-doubt rather than self-enhancement from postmodernist insights?

For example, recall that I (Sherryl) almost disqualified my criticisms of the Wholeness Center as personal projections. Losing some of my postmodern doubt allowed me to accept my righteous indignation and let it direct me to an analysis of unjust arrangements. Writer bell hooks (1990) observed that some of the postmodern buzzwords regarding race make social criticism less likely:

> *Other* and *difference* are taking the place of commonly known words deemed uncool or too simplistic, words like *oppression*, *exploitation*, and *domination*. . . . There would be no need, however, for any unruly radical black folks to raise critical objections . . . if all this passionate focus on race were not so neatly divorced from a recognition of racism, of the continuing domination of blacks by whites, and (to use some of those out-of-date uncool terms) of the continued suffering and pain in black life. (pp. 51-52)

It is possible to recognize the constructed nature of our work without having it muddy our critical eye. Becoming aware of how authors represent others can sensitize us to the operation of power.

IDENTITY AND COMMUNITY

"Ethnographic writing tends to be surprisingly boring," Mary Louise Pratt (1986, p. 33) told us. She asked, "How . . . could such interesting people doing such interesting things produce such dull books? What did they have to do to themselves?" (p. 33).

Fieldworkers, like many professionals, learn to ignore or hide their troubling feelings and write their reports in a language that masks subjectivity. Instead, we call for a new professional, one who recognizes, along with Ben Agger (1991), that we should put our empirical claims to the test of "rigorous self-reflection and self-criticism" (p. 111).

Will an identity of difference alienate us further from mainstream social scientists? In our experience, quantitative researchers already think of what we do (and who we are) as "different." Why spend time trying to refute that perception? Claiming the strengths of our method and the uniqueness of our identity will make us into better fieldworkers and make it easier for us to talk back to the positivist voices in our heads or in our hallways.

We call for an identity anchored to our analytic assumptions rather than to immersion. Letting go of immersion as the basis of our identity will make us think twice about separating data collection and analysis. Having an analytically based identity might also lead us to recognize and seek out colleagues in other disciplines. Fieldworkers will discover, as we did, that scholars in a variety of fields share our assumptions. We have, for example, found like-minded people in cultural studies, education, geography, oral history, performance studies, folklore, English, communication, nursing, and public health. Those who use historical methods, oral histories, and narratives confront similar analytic and methodological problems. Knowing we are part of a shared tradition that crosses disciplinary boundaries lessens our feelings of marginality and strengthens our resolve.

Fieldworkers must build a community of sentiment, with local and long-distance members, that opposes the competitive individualism of academia. The lone scholar is a sociological impossibility. Our "individual" works rely on language, literatures, and feedback from colleagues (Becker, 1986). Yet researchers believe that talking to others about their problems will make them vulnerable to charges of incompetence or weakness.

Let us acknowledge our *inter*dependence. We can give up the individualist model and instead create interdisciplinary networks and informal groups that encourage us to give and receive intellectual and emotional support. In our experience, having cooperative contexts in which to think, talk, and write makes us work better and feel better.

6. APPENDIX

To be able to trust yet to be skeptical of your own experience, I have come to believe, is one mark of the mature workman [or -woman]. This ambiguous confidence is indispensable to originality in any intellectual pursuit, and the file [of self-reflective notes] is one way by which you can develop and justify such confidence.

C. Wright Mills (1959, p. 197)

Putting Emotions Into Fieldnotes

How can we put our emotions and analyses into our notes? We must do the impossible and start before we begin. Before making that first phone call or visit, freewrite (see Elbow, 1981): Write fast and furiously without worrying about spelling or grammar or coherence. Ask yourself, What images do I hold of the people and the place I am about to study and how do I feel about those images? How did I come to study this setting at this time?

Ask yourself about the needs you expect this setting to fulfill: Do I have an axe to grind? Do I have a mission? Am I looking for a cause or a community? Do I expect this study to help me resolve personal problems? Am I hoping to create a different self? What political assumptions do I have? What kinds of setting activities or subgroups might I avoid or discount because of who I am or what I believe? As you collect data, freewrite about discrepancies between your expectations of the people and the place and your early observations in the field (see also Geer, 1967; Kleinman, 1980; Krieger, 1985).

What do we do once we are in the field? Typically, we ignore ourselves and put all our efforts into watching and listening to those we study. Instead, assume you are a full-fledged participant in the setting. It does not matter how little time you have spent in the field. Once you are there, you are a part of it. Try this: Write your notes as if you were someone else observing the setting. That fieldworker would note what you said and did and ask you how you feel and what you think. You must treat yourself this way.

Put your reactions, as much as possible, into your fieldnotes. If you felt angry about what a participant said, then write about that reaction immediately after putting the quote from that person on paper. You might choose to make a short note, especially if you are not sure what you were feeling: "I felt uneasy. I wanted to move away from him. I am not sure why."

Once you have finished writing your notes, put them away for a day or so. At that time you are ready to write "notes-on-notes." Read your fieldnotes, elaborate on the emotions you mentioned in the notes, and write about why you think you had them. What assumptions underlie those reactions? What do these feelings tell you about you? About your role in the setting? About other participants' roles? About fieldwork? You might discover that you have idealistic notions about the method that you can release.

As you read your notes, think about the tone you used. Did you sound distant or engaged, sarcastic or sympathetic, happy or sad? Did you seem conflicted, defensive, secretive, or estranged? Did your reactions differ from those you had in previous notes? In what ways? Occasionally, ask yourself, What changes have I noticed, in myself and in participants, so far? If you address this question as you write notes-on-notes you will bring earlier sets of notes into your ongoing analysis.

No matter how extensive your fieldnotes, you should always have at least two sets of notes per time: the notes you wrote shortly after the field visit or interview and your commentary (notes-on-notes). Do not go back to the field until you have made some sense of your previous set of notes, *in writing*. Learn to have a sense of incompletion about your notes until you have exhausted your thoughts on paper.

Create or join a group whose members share your worldview (see chapter 5). Think about including people from other disciplines. Whether or not you call yourselves a writing group, it is helpful to read your writing out loud and get feedback on how others hear your words (see Elbow, 1973, for a model). Read some of your fieldnotes or analytic notes to the group. Ask them to listen for the assumptions embedded in your account. It is difficult to become aware of all that you feel and you might be embarrassed about some of the feelings you know about. Let others pick up on your attitude, mood, or tone as you read. They will help you improve your work and dispel some of your anxiety about doing justice to the project.

What follows is an example of Martha's fieldnotes and analytic commentary. The incident occurred 6 weeks into the fieldwork. We expanded on her notes-on-notes to give you a range of the kinds of things you can include. But this account is abbreviated, so think about how you would interpret the incident and what you would add to the notes-on-notes.

Fieldnotes

Tissy, a supervisor, asked me to "keep an eye on things" while the staff attended a short meeting. Roseann, an employee, talked excitedly to me about the new apartment she'd soon move into. I turned to Belinda (another employee) and said, "Do you get to move to an apartment, too?" Belinda shook her head, her eyes welling up with tears. I said, "Oh, I'm sorry I asked, Belinda!" Her head sagged, but I could still see her eyes getting red. Roseann said, "I can't wait!" I quickly cautioned her, "Roseann, maybe you shouldn't talk about this right now." Roseann kept smiling; she seemed oblivious to what I'd just said.

I was pretty nervous. I didn't know how to make Belinda feel better. I was worried she'd get more upset and create a scene, forcing Tissy to leave her meeting. Tissy might get mad at me for what happened; it would be my fault. But I tried not to show Belinda that I was nervous.

Belinda stopped working. I said in a kind voice, "Try not to think about it right now. Don't cry." Emily, another employee, asked, "Belinda, what's the matter?" Belinda didn't say anything, but she looked terribly sad. Emily walked around the table, bent down next to Belinda, and said in a concerned tone, "Belinda, what's the matter? Is someone bothering you?" Belinda nodded. Emily asked, "Is it Marka?" When Emily suggested this, she gestured in the direction of Marka Bradley, who worked at the other end of the workshop. Belinda nodded, looking miserable. Emily said in a firm, sympathetic tone, "Don't cry, Belinda!" Then she turned and quietly walked to Tissy's desk and got a tissue. She came back and said, "Here, Belinda." Belinda took the tissue and dried her eyes and blew her nose. Emily patted her back.

I said to Roseann, "Does Marka live in the same place as you?" Roseann said, "No, she lives in the Oak home with . . . ." After a few moments, Belinda calmed down. I smiled at her, trying to give her a comforting look. I felt relieved that she was calm and that maybe I wasn't completely responsible for her tears.

Notes-on-Notes

When Belinda started to cry, I assumed I understood her distress. I figured she felt excluded from the adventure of moving into an apartment and out of the group home. I also assumed she was jealous of Roseann, her current housemate. I wished I'd been sensitive to Belinda's exclusion and I regretted my question. Thus I asked Roseann to drop the subject because I didn't want her to upset Belinda further.

My jealousy hypothesis was thrown off when Emily appeared and suggested that Marka was bothering Belinda. I'd been at the workshop all morning and hadn't seen the two of them interact or exchange looks. I asked Roseann where Marka lived in case they'd argued at home before work, but discovered they didn't live together. I was baffled. I can't know what went through Belinda's mind without asking her, but I have to admit I feel ambivalent about it. What if she got upset again? Why do I get so upset at that thought? Well, there's no way around this. I'll have to talk to her and think about who else to probe about what's going on.

The responsibility I felt was tremendous. I don't think it's only because I thought I made someone cry, which violates my sense of myself as a good person. I think it was partly a function of my *role*—quasi-supervisor. No one told me I'd be responsible for employees' emotional upsets while the staff were gone, but I felt responsible because of the position I'd accepted. This sense of responsibility made me feel nervous and worried. Like a good person-in-charge, I didn't share my anxiety with Belinda. I wanted to appear as a responsible person, as someone in the know. But not showing my vulnerability in all this kept me as a "superior," something that contradicts what I think I want to be—a friend to employees, or at least more of a peer. Then there's the matter of emotional labor, my own and Emily's. I felt at a loss; I really wasn't sure how to deal with the situation. Should I be deeply sympathetic? Ignore the whole thing? I did what I'd seen staff members do. I told Belinda to use what sociologists of emotions would call a cognitive strategy, to stop thinking about the upsetting thought. I also gave Belinda a behavioral strategy by telling her not to cry. I'm writing as if I gave her these strategies as gifts, so she could help herself. But I could interpret my actions less generously and say that I was using strategies that would *control* her behavior and made *me* feel better. After all, I was worried that the staff would think me irresponsible, hence my great relief when she stopped crying. Do staff members mostly control employees? Does emotional labor become a means of social control in this setting?

Like the staff, I didn't ask Belinda what was wrong. Instead, I instantly tried to calm her down, as if getting rid of the outburst was the important thing, not dealing with what I'd said that might have caused it or finding out what was on her mind. This is something I've noticed that staff members do. They don't concentrate on what's upsetting the employee; they jump right into controlling the outburst. Nor have I seen them talk about the content of the incident with the employee later, when he or she has calmed down.

Why didn't I let Belinda cry? Didn't the "Don't cry" message delegitimate her feelings? Why tell her not to think about something upsetting? Maybe she needed to work through whatever was bothering her. I don't usually appreciate it when someone tells *me* to calm down when I'm upset. If I'm angry at that person, I usually want to talk about it.

This incident raises a lot of questions about the staff and the employees. Do the staff have this strong sense of responsibility for employees' emotional responses (as I did)? Do the staff blame themselves when things get "out of control"? Did my reactions mirror those of a novice staff member?

I gave an apology of sorts to Belinda when I said, "I'm sorry I asked, Belinda!" Do staff ever do that? Or do they normalize outbursts and lose a sense of responsibility? My guess is that they eventually dissociate themselves from blame. They start to believe that "So-and-So is like that." Or they believe that someone with this particular disorder gets upset randomly, so they don't have to take responsibility for causing any particular outburst. Yet staff members can still feel responsible for failing to keep the peace, regardless of what triggered the incident.

What about employees' emotion work? Emily worked on Belinda and she seemed good at it, better than me. Did she learn those lessons from the staff? Do employees ever feel responsible for their peers' outbursts? In what situations do they do emotion work on each other? Do their strategies differ from the staff's? Is emotion work status-enhancing for employees (perhaps they think of it as adult behavior)? When do employees resist their peers' emotion work (perhaps they find it patronizing)? When do employees resist the staff's emotional labor? Do staff members notice the emotion work employees practice among themselves, and if so, do they approve?

Which emotions do staff find acceptable? Do they approve of sadness more than anger? Which emotional displays do staff condone? Are tears more acceptable than punching a wall? These questions might tap into the culture of emotions in the workshop.

And so on.

REFERENCES

Abbott, A. (1981). Status and status strain in the professions. *American Journal of Sociology*, *86*, 819-835.

Adler, P., & Adler, P. (1987). *Membership roles in field research*. Newbury Park, CA: Sage.

Agger, B. (1991). Critical theory, poststructuralism, postmodernism: Their sociological relevance. *Annual Review of Sociology*, *17*, 105-131.

Athens, L. H. (1989). *The creation of dangerous violent criminals*. London: Routledge.

Atkinson, P. (1992). *Understanding ethnographic texts*. Newbury Park, CA: Sage.

Becker, H. S. (1963). *Outsiders*. New York: Free Press.

Becker, H. S. (1970a). Interviewing medical students. In W. J. Filstead (Ed.), *Qualitative methodology* (pp. 103-106). Chicago: Rand-McNally.

Becker, H. S. (1970b). The nature of a profession. In H. S. Becker, *Sociological work: Method and substance* (pp. 87-103). New Brunswick, NJ: Transaction Books.

Becker, H. S. (1986). *Writing for social scientists: How to start and finish your thesis, book, or article*. Chicago: University of Chicago Press.

Becker, H. S., Gordon, A. C., & LeBailly, R. K. (1984). Fieldwork with the computer: Criteria for analyzing systems. *Qualitative Sociology*, *7*(1-2), 16-33.

Berger, B. (1981). *The survival of a counterculture: Ideological work and everyday life among rural communards*. Berkeley: University of California Press.

Blumer, H. (1969). *Symbolic interactionism: Perspective and method*. Englewood Cliffs, NJ: Prentice-Hall.

Bourgois, P. (1990). Confronting anthropological ethics: Ethnographic lessons from Central America. *Journal of Peace Research*, *27*(1), 43-54.

Burawoy, M., Burton, A., Ferguson, A. A., Fox, K. J., Gamson, J., Gartrell, N., Hurst, L., Kurzman, C., Salzinger, L., Schiffman, J., & Ui, S. (1991). *Ethnography unbound: Power and resistance in the modern metropolis*. Berkeley: University of California Press.

Cesara, M. (1982). *Reflections of a woman anthropologist: No hiding place*. New York: Academic Press.

Charmaz, K. (1990). "Discovering" chronic illness: Using grounded theory. *Social Science and Medicine*, *11*, 1161-1172.

Clark, C. (1987). Sympathy biography and sympathy margin. *American Journal of Sociology*, *93*, 290-321.

Clifford, J., & Marcus, G. E. (Eds.). (1986). *Writing culture: The poetics and politics of ethnography*. Berkeley: University of California Press.

Conaway, M. E. (1986). The pretense of the neutral observer. In T. L. Whitehead & M. E. Conaway (Eds.), *Self, sex, and gender in cross-cultural fieldwork* (pp. 52-63). Urbana: University of Illinois Press.

Corsino, L. (1987). Fieldworker blues: Emotional stress and research underinvolvement in fieldwork settings. *Social Science Journal*, *24*, 275-285.

Daniels, A. K. (1983). Self-deception and self-discovery in fieldwork. *Qualitative Sociology*, *6*, 195-214.

Daniels, A. K. (1988). *Invisible careers: Civic leaders from the volunteer world*. Chicago: University of Chicago Press.

Davis, F. (1974). Stories and sociology. *Urban Life*, *3*, 310-316.

Devereux, G. (1967). *From anxiety to method in the behavioral sciences*. New York: Humanities Press.

DeVita, P. R. (Ed.). (1990). *The humbled anthropologist: Tales from the Pacific*. Belmont, CA: Wadsworth.

di Leonardo, M. (1987). Oral history as ethnographic encounter. *Oral History Review, 15*, 1-20.

Douglas, J. D. (1976). *Investigative social research*. Beverly Hills, CA: Sage.

Dunn, L. (1991). Research alert! Qualitative research may be hazardous to your health! *Qualitative Health Research, 1*, 388-392.

Elbow, P. (1973). *Writing without teachers*. New York: Oxford University Press.

Elbow, P. (1981). *Writing with power: Techniques for mastering the writing process*. New York: Oxford University Press.

Ellis, C. (1991). Sociological introspection and emotional experience. *Symbolic Interaction, 14*(1), 23-50.

Estroff, S. (1981). *Making it crazy*. Berkeley: University of California Press.

Fee, E. (1988). Critiques of modern science: The relationship of feminism to other radical epistemologies. In R. Bleier (Ed.), *Feminist approaches to science* (pp. 42-56). Elmsford, NY: Pergamon.

Fine, G. A. (1992, August). *Ten lies of ethnography*. Paper presented at the annual meeting of the American Sociological Association, Pittsburgh, PA.

Fine, G. A., & Martin, D. D. (1990). Sarcasm, satire, and irony as voices in Erving Goffman's *Asylums*. *Journal of Contemporary Ethnography, 19*, 89-115.

Flax, J. (1987). Postmodernism and gender relations in feminist theory. *Signs, 12*, 621-43.

Fox, R. (1979). The autopsy: Its place in the attitude-learning of second year medical students. In R. Fox (Ed.), *Essays in medical sociology* (pp. 51-77). New York: Wiley.

Gans, H. J. (1982). *The urban villagers: Group and class in the life of Italian-Americans*. New York: Free Press.

Geer, B. (1967). First days in the field. In P. E. Hammond (Ed.), *Sociologists at work* (pp. 372-398). Garden City, NY: Doubleday.

Gilligan, C. (1982). *In a different voice*. Cambridge, MA: Harvard University Press.

Glaser, B. G., & Strauss, A. L. (1967). *The discovery of grounded theory: Strategies for qualitative research*. New York: Aldine.

Goffman, E. (1961). *Asylums*. Garden City, NY: Anchor.

Goffman, E. (1989). On fieldwork. *Journal of Contemporary Ethnography, 18*, 123-132.

Goldfarb, J. (1991). *The cynical society*. Chicago: University of Chicago Press.

Gordon, D. F. (1987). Getting close by staying distant: Fieldwork with proselytizing groups. *Qualitative Sociology, 10*, 267-287.

Granovetter, M. (1984). Small is bountiful: Labor markets and establishment size. *American Sociological Review, 49*, 323-334.

Gusfield, J. (1976). The literary rhetoric of science: Comedy and pathos in drinking-driving research. *American Sociological Review, 41*, 16-34.

Hammersley, M., & Atkinson, P. (1983). *Ethnography: Principles in practice*. New York: Tavistock.

Hill, R. P., & Stamey, M. (1990). The homeless in America: An examination of possessions and consumption behavior. *Journal of Consumer Research, 17*, 303-321.

Hochschild, A. R. (1983). *The managed heart: Commercialization of human feeling*. Berkeley: University of California Press.

65

hooks, b. (1990). Critical interrogation: Talking race, resisting racism. In b. hooks, *Yearning: Race, gender, and cultural politics* (pp. 51-55). Boston: South End Press.

Horowitz, R. (1986). Remaining an outsider: Membership as a threat to research rapport. *Journal of Contemporary Ethnography, 14,* 409-430.

Hunt, J. C. (1989). *Psychoanalytic aspects of fieldwork.* Newbury Park, CA: Sage.

Hunter, A. (Ed.). (1990). *The rhetoric of social research: Understood and believed.* New Brunswick, NJ: Rutgers University Press.

Jackson, J. E. (1986). On trying to be an Amazon. In T. L. Whitehead & M. E. Conaway (Eds.), *Self, sex, and gender in cross-cultural fieldwork* (pp. 263-274). Urbana: University of Illinois Press.

Jackson, J. E. (1990a). "Dejà entendu": The liminal qualities of anthropological fieldnotes. *Journal of Contemporary Ethnography, 19,* 8-43.

Jackson, J. E. (1990b). "I am a fieldnote": Fieldnotes as a symbol of professional identity. In R. Sanjek (Ed.), *Fieldnotes: The makings of anthropology* (pp. 3-33). Ithaca, NY: Cornell University Press.

Jaggar, A. M. (1989). Love and knowledge: Emotion in feminist epistemology. In A. M. Jaggar & S. R. Bordo (Eds.), *Gender/body/knowledge: Feminist reconstructions of being and knowing* (pp. 145-171). New Brunswick, NJ: Rutgers University Press.

Johnson, J. M. (1975). *Doing field research.* New York: Free Press.

Jules-Rosette, B. (1975). *African apostles: Ritual and conversion in the church of John Maranke.* Ithaca, NY: Cornell University Press.

Kanter, R. M. (1977). *Men and women of the corporation.* New York: Basic Books.

Karp, D. A. (1980). Observing behavior in public places: Problems and strategies. In W. B. Shaffir, R. A. Stebbins & A. Turowetz (Eds.), *Fieldwork experience: Qualitative approaches to social research* (pp. 82-97). New York: St. Martins Press.

Kleinman, S. (1980). Learning the ropes as fieldwork analysis. In W. B. Shaffir, R. A. Stebbins, & A. Turowetz (Eds.), *Fieldwork experience: Qualitative approaches to social research* (pp. 171-183). New York: St. Martins Press.

Kleinman, S. (1984). *Equals before God: Seminarians as humanistic professionals.* Chicago: University of Chicago Press.

Kleinman, S. (1991). Field-workers' feelings: What we feel, who we are, how we analyze. In W. B. Shaffir & R. A. Stebbins (Eds.), *Experiencing fieldwork: An inside view of qualitative research* (pp. 184-195). Newbury Park, CA: Sage.

Kleinman, S., Copp, M. A., & Henderson, K. (1992). *Qualitatively different: Teaching field work to graduate students.* Manuscript submitted for publication.

Koonz, C. (1987). *Mothers in the fatherland: Women, the family, and Nazi politics.* New York: St. Martins Press.

Krieger, S. (1985). Beyond subjectivity: The use of the self in social science. *Qualitative Sociology, 8,* 309-324.

Krieger, S. (1991). *Social science and the self: Personal essays on an art form.* New Brunswick, NJ: Rutgers University Press.

Lofland, J., & Lofland, L. H. (1984). *Analyzing social settings: A guide to qualitative observation and analysis.* Belmont, CA: Wadsworth.

Lutz, C. (1988). *Unnatural emotions.* Chicago: University of Chicago Press.

Marshall, M. (1990). Two tales from the Trukese taproom. In P. R. DeVita (Ed.), *The humbled anthropologist: Tales from the Pacific* (pp. 12-17). Belmont, CA: Wadsworth.

Mascia-Lees, F. E., Sharpe, P., & Cohen, C. B. (1989). The postmodernist turn in anthropology: Cautions from a feminist perspective. *Signs, 15*, 7-33.

Mead, G. H. (1934). *Mind, self, and society.* Chicago: University of Chicago Press.

Miller, J. B. (1976). *Toward a new psychology of women.* Boston: Beacon.

Miller, S. M. (1952). The participant observer and "over-rapport." *American Sociological Review, 17*, 97-99.

Mills, C. W. (1959). *The sociological imagination.* New York: Oxford University Press.

Mills, T., & Kleinman, S. (1988). Emotions, reflexivity, and action: An interactionist analysis. *Social Forces, 66*, 1009-1027.

Mitchell, R. G., Jr. (1991). Secrecy and disclosure in fieldwork. In W. B. Shaffir & R. A. Stebbins (Eds.), *Experiencing fieldwork: An inside view of qualitative research* (pp. 97-108). Newbury Park, CA: Sage.

Nash, J. (1990). Working at and working: Computer fritters. *Journal of Contemporary Ethnography, 19*(2), 207-225.

Neitz, M. J., & Spickard, J. V. (1990). Steps toward a sociology of religious experience: The theories of Mihaly Csikszentmihalyi and Alfred Schutz. *Sociological Analysis, 51*(1), 15-33.

O'Connor, F. (1971). *The complete stories.* New York: Farrar, Straus & Giroux.

Ottenberg, S. (1990). Thirty years of fieldnotes: Changing relationships to the text. In R. Sanjek (Ed.), *Fieldnotes: The makings of anthropology* (pp. 139-160). Ithaca, NY: Cornell University Press.

Peshkin, A. (1988). Virtuous subjectivity: In the participant-observer's I's. In D. N. Berg & K. K. Smith (Eds.), *The self in social inquiry: Researching methods* (pp. 267-281). Newbury Park, CA: Sage.

Platt, J. (1976). *Realities of social research.* New York: John Wiley.

Pollner, M., & Emerson, R. M. (1983). The dynamics of inclusion and distance in fieldwork relations. In R. M. Emerson (Ed.), *Contemporary field research* (pp. 235-252). Boston: Little, Brown.

Polsky, N. (1967). *Hustlers, beats and others.* Chicago: Aldine.

Pratt, M. L. (1986). Fieldwork in common places. In J. Clifford & G. E. Marcus (Eds.), *Writing culture: The poetics and politics of ethnography* (pp. 27-50). Berkeley: University of California Press.

Punch, M. (1986). *The politics and ethics of fieldwork.* Newbury Park, CA: Sage.

Punch, M. (1989). Researching police deviance: A personal encounter with the limitations and liabilities of field-work. *British Journal of Sociology, 40*(2), 177-204.

Reinharz, S. (1979). *On becoming a social scientist.* San Francisco: Jossey-Bass.

Reinharz, S. (1992). *Feminist methods in social research.* New York: Oxford University Press.

Riesman, D., & Watson, J. (1967). The sociability project: A chronicle of frustration and achievement. In P. E. Hammond (Ed.), *Sociologists at work* (pp. 270-371). Garden City, NY: Doubleday.

Rosaldo, R. (1989). *Culture and truth.* Boston: Beacon.

Rose, D. (1990). *Living the ethnographic life.* Newbury Park, CA: Sage.

Rosenhan, D. L. (1988). On being sane in insane places. In C. Clark & H. Robboy (Eds.), *Social interaction: Readings in sociology* (pp. 304-322). New York: St. Martins Press.

Roth, P. A. (1989). Ethnography without tears. *Current Anthropology, 30*, 555-569.

Rothman, B. K. (1986). Reflections: On hard work. *Qualitative Sociology, 9*, 48-53.

Rothschild, J., & Whitt, J. A. (1986). *The cooperative workplace*. Cambridge, MA: Cambridge University Press.

Sanders, C. (1980). Rope burns: Impediments to the achievement of basic comfort early in the field research experience. In W. B. Shaffir, R. A. Stebbins, & A. Turowetz (Eds.), *Fieldwork experience: Qualitative approaches to social research* (pp. 158-171). New York: St. Martins Press.

Scully, D. (1990). *Understanding sexual violence: A study of convicted rapists*. Boston, MA: Unwin Hyman.

Shaffir, W. B., & Stebbins, R. A. (Eds.). (1991). *Experiencing fieldwork: An inside view of qualitative research*. Newbury Park, CA: Sage.

Smith, A. C., III, & Kleinman, S. (1989). Managing emotions in medical school: Students' contacts with the living and the dead. *Social Psychology Quarterly, 52*, 56-69.

Stack, C. (1974). *All our kin: Strategies for survival in a black community*. New York: Harper & Row.

Tallerico, M. (1991). Applications of qualitative analysis software: A view from the field. *Qualitative Sociology, 14*, 275-285.

Taylor, S. J. (1987). Observing abuse: Professional ethics and personal morality in field research. *Qualitative Sociology, 10*, 288-302.

Thoits, P. A. (1985). Self-labeling processes in mental illness: The role of emotional deviance. *American Journal of Sociology, 91*, 221-249.

Thorne, B. (1983). Political activist as participant observer: Conflicts of commitment in a study of the draft resistance movement of the 1960s. In R. M. Emerson (Ed.), *Contemporary field research* (pp. 216-234). Boston: Little, Brown.

Van Maanen, J. (1979). The moral fix: On the ethics of field work. In P. K. Manning & R. N. Smith (Eds.), *Social science methods* (Vol. 1, pp. 115-139). New York: Irvington.

Van Maanen, J. (1988). *Tales of the field: On writing ethnography*. Chicago: University of Chicago Press.

Warren, C.A.B. (1988). *Gender issues in field research*. Newbury Park, CA: Sage.

Whitehead, T. A., & Conaway, M. E. (Eds.). (1986). *Self, sex, and gender in cross-cultural fieldwork*. Urbana: University of Illinois Press.

Whyte, W. F. (1955). *Streetcorner society: The social structure of an Italian slum*. Chicago: University of Chicago Press.

Wolf, M. (1992). *A thrice-told tale: Feminism, postmodernism and ethnographic responsibility*. Stanford, CA: Stanford University Press.

ABOUT THE AUTHORS

SHERRYL KLEINMAN is Associate Professor of Sciology at the University of North Carolina, Chapel Hill. She is author of *Equals Before God: Seminarians as Humanistic Professionals* (1984, University of Chicago Press) and articles on symbolic interaction, sociology of emotions, gender identity, socialization, and qualitative methods. She is completing a book on the construction of inequalities in an alternative organization.

MARTHA A. COPP is a doctoral candidate in the Department of Sociology at the University of North Carolina, Chapel Hill. Her research interests are in the sociology of emotions, qualitative methods, socialization, and work and occupations. She is completing her dissertation, "Raising Adults: Social Control and Emotion Management in a Sheltered Workshop."